BOCCONI
UNIVERSITY
PRESS

Francesco Pagano · Luca Zerbini

STANDING UP FOR THE PLANET

45 Stories of Extraordinary Women
Who Are Changing the World

The realization of this volume was also made possible by

Cover: Cristina Bernasconi, Milan
Typesetting: Laura Panigara, Cesano Boscone (MI)

EGEA S.p.A.
Via Salasco, 5 - 20136 Milano
Tel. 02/5836.5751 – Fax 02/5836.5753
egea.edizioni@unibocconi.it – www.egeaeditore.it

First edition: November 2023

ISBN Domestic Edition	979-12-80623-27-0
ISBN International Edition	978-88-31322-99-7
ISBN Digital Domestic Edition	978-88-238-8736-7
ISBN Digital International Edition	978-88-31322-29-4

Print: Logo s.r.l., Borgoricco (PD)

Table of contents

Foreword

Riccardo Valentini[*]

According to the IPCC's Sixth Assessment Report (AR6), atmospheric concentrations of green house gases (GHGs) are at their highest in 800,000 years. In the last fifty years alone, GHG emissions have increased 2.5 times, freshwater withdrawal has doubled, and the availability of agricultural land per capita has halved (from 1.4 to 0.7 hectares). This is unprecedented. Each single year between 2015 and 2020 was warmer than any previous year for which records exist. The year 2023 is shaping up to be among the ten warmest years on record.

The rate of the warming-up of our planet has accelerated since the 1980s, compared with the previous eighty years. Overall, temperatures have risen faster than in any previous IPCC assessment cycle. AR6 states that "observed changes in the atmosphere, oceans, cryosphere and biosphere provide unequivocal evidence of a warming world." Since the beginning of the current century, all key indicators of the climate system have been increasing at levels not seen in centuries, or millennia, and are changing at rates unprecedented in at least the last 2,000 years.

In particular, the global mean surface temperature increased by 1.09°C between the pre-industrial reference period of 1850–1900 and the decade 2011–20. This was most likely the warmest period in about 125,000 years. The Earth will be 1.4 to 4.4°C warmer than pre-industrial levels by the end of this century. In addition, the 1.5 and 2°C limits of the Paris Agreement will be violated unless there are rapid and rigorous cuts in emissions of CO_2 and other GHGs. The last time the global surface temperature was at or above 2.5°C higher than in 1850–1900 was more than 3 million years ago.

Climate change is affecting several global critical sectors: agriculture, biodiversity, freshwater, and oceans; and it is augmenting the vulnerability

---

[*] Professor of Forest Ecology, University of Tuscia (Italy), 2007 Peace Nobel Prize recipient (together with IPCC)

of less developed countries. For example, the agri-food sector uses about 80% of the world's freshwater, 30% of the world's energy, and it represents more than 37% of manmade GHG emissions, including indirect emissions, such as those from deforestation.

In some regions of the world, such as the tropics and parts of the temperate regions, increased climate extremes will negatively affect the agriculture, forestry, and fisheries sectors, with a 35% yield reduction in African countries and a 2% reduction globally, per each decade, while food demand is increasing.

At the same time, we expect deadly extreme weather events around the world to increase significantly. The middle of 2021 saw, for example, a record-breaking 'heat bubble' in the Pacific Northwest, wildfires in the western parts of the United States and Europe, catastrophic floods in Europe and China, and rain-induced landslides in India. Finally, intensive floods in 2023 hit the Emilia Romagna region of Italy.

The AR6 says it is virtually certain that "the frequency and intensity of warm extremes have increased and those of cold extremes have decreased on a global scale since 1950." As for extreme precipitation' events, the report concludes that their frequency and intensity "are likely to have increased on a global scale in most terrestrial regions with good observational coverage. Human influence is probably the main driver."

Climate change is causing ice and snow to melt across most of the planet. During the decades 1979–88 and 2010–19, the average monthly August–October area of the Arctic sea ice has shrunk by about a quarter, resulting in the loss of about 2 million square kilometers of ice. In addition, rising temperatures led to a shift from thick, multi-year ice to thinner, younger ice. While multi-year ice made up about one-third of the Arctic sea ice coverage in March 1985, multi-year ice was only at 1.2% in March 2019, according to the report. The loss of multi-year sea ice was particularly rapid during the 2000s.

At the same time, climate change and migration are interconnected and complex issues that will have significant implications for individuals, communities, and countries around the world. Climate change can lead to environmental degradation, such as rising sea levels, extreme weather events, droughts, and desertification. These environmental changes can make certain areas uninhabitable or less suitable for human habitation, forcing people to move in search of better living conditions. In some cases, climate change can directly or indirectly contribute to forced displacements of entire communities. People may be displaced by events such as hurricanes, floods, or wildfires. Slow-onset changes, such as prolonged droughts or sea-level rise, can also make living conditions unsustainable, leading to migration as the only means for survival.

So, what do we do now?

Given the critical tipping point on the climate system and its impact on the world, what are the solutions and actions that could save all of us, as well as future generations?

First, we must react quickly to make our society more resilient to climate change. By 2030, most likely, we will reach between +1.5 and 2°C vs. today, which is the maximum limit possible to prevent dramatic changes. The time is now to invest in adaptation measures. 'Adaptation' means to address climate change by building more secure infrastructures; to promote better water management, coastal protection, land use planning, agricultural adaptation, ecosystem restoration; and to develop early warning systems and provide heat mitigation, health adaptation, and community engagement solutions.

Second, we must stabilize the climate through the end of the century by reducing GHG emissions and increasing carbon sequestration. Renewable energies, energy efficiency, and electrical mobility can have a significant impact on reaching the goal of reducing emissions by 90% by 2050 (as supported also by the European Union), but, still, it will not be enough. We need to reach, at the same time, net zero emissions (carbon neutrality), which can only be achieved by the biological sequestration of carbon dioxide, namely planting new trees, and capturing carbon in the agricultural soil. The challenge in front of us is to react as quickly as possible, via the implementation of global, national, and regional policies, while leveraging already available solutions and testing new ones that are still to come. The time is now!

The factory of life

Francesco Pagano[*]

The aim of this book is bold: nothing short of changing the entire conversation on how to save the planet. To do that, we should change the way we look at ourselves.

In the Foreword, Professor Riccardo Valentini tells us that there is a clear target on temperature and emissions reduction for the next few decades. This is non-negotiable if we want to survive as a community and as a species.

How do we stimulate radical change in the hearts of all human beings, companies, and institutions? We need all hands on deck and to have a lot of forgiveness for what has been done in the past, if we don't want to get stuck in a blame game or in the usual divide between two opposing fronts, that is, pro vs. contra the so-called green revolution. I do not believe the root cause of the current dire straits is a plot by an elite of ultra-rich or ultra-conservatives who want our planet to implode. Change is complex. Even though we know what to do – cut emissions and reach carbon neutrality – there is very often a political and, I would say, real fear that too fast of a revolution will disrupt society, with consequences that are impossible to estimate for any CEO or government. The material incentives to make a U-turn are not there yet. What happens if unemployment rises dramatically when we curb demand for strategic industries such as the fossil fuel-based sectors of our global market? Who will suffer the most if we consume less of what we love, from fashion accessories to mobility network services, from energy to housing development, all of them based on traditional supply chain models? These are the most difficult questions in history, and the answers are unfortunately difficult to untangle. What's necessary is an unprecedented amount of technology and imagination, strategy, and perfect execution. For

---

[*] Senior Partner, Jakala

this reason, it felt natural to ask the doers to share a slice of their life. It felt
especially natural to engage women who have experienced painful personal
and professional journeys and who have finally landed in a place where
pivoting their existence in a brave new way was the only reasonable choice.
We needed to ask the human beings who are best at carrying the weight of
society and the light of a different future. We wanted forty-five life stories.
They had to be women, at least in our opinion. Reading their stories is a
true gift. There is a common thread across these leaders, which feels very
much like action and rebirth.

Our land is our factory

The first message that comes out of the book is that we do not have to go
back to a past state of supposed purity. That imaginary locus does not exist
and never will. We have obviously raised the temperature of the planet too
much compared with pre-industrial levels. The way to go is not backward,
but forward. Our land is a factory, so to speak, and it needs to remain one.
Change will require 'factories,' namely some tangible *facere,* which is the
Latin word behind the term. The key to success is to use our human, in-
tellectual, and technological capital to continue shaping our world. Mother
earth will keep being a worksite, and there is nothing more exciting than
rethinking the way we live our world: traveling, eating, clothing ourselves,
loving, and having fun. There is no Garden of Eden that we need to restore.
Our role as a global community is to transform and humanize our land. If
there is an essential feature for the future CEO or head of state, it is continuous action. The women of this book have an irresistible urge to move and
fabricate a different world, be it through impact investing or food making,
researching or teaching, leading a start-up or a corporate organization. The
reader will notice the doubts and fears of these change makers and will be
drawn into the magic of forty-five spirits who decided that the weight of
not doing anything was unbearable. Imagining a different future entails,
first, relentless and stubborn trial and error. The future belongs to those
who will take a leap of faith. The next generations will thank those who decided to step out of the status quo and challenge the unknown despite their
fear, or who went above and beyond rational behaviors such as the mantra
of solid returns on investment or the preservation of self-interest. Payback
is, of course, an important prerequisite of any intelligent program, but the
starting point for today's leaders is an urgent bias for *facere,* which is action,
without waiting for the perfect conditions, the right wind, or a blue ocean
of infinite growth.

Our land is our life

The second key element of the book is that this is a war that we will not win once and for all. Our land is a living environment. We must treat our resources like a living body that is continuously evolving. This flux requires accurate measurements and ever-moving adaptations of our strategic choices. Giving birth to a new state of the world is just a first step into a new era of perpetual nurturing, caring, forgiving, and growing together. This is what we do in life. We don't manage our planet like a project or treat it like a possession or an object. We carry the responsibility to keep the biosphere and the human sphere alive and well. The future belongs to the heroes that look at our world as something that needs to be kept alive, at any cost. Life is the most important value in our books, reports, and scores. Future generations will thank the life lovers and not the savvy businesspeople. Giving birth requires courage. There is a lot of talk these days around artificial intelligence and the ability of machines to sift through our past data to generate suggestions, recommendations, and sometimes automated decisions. Looking at the past can be dangerous and saddening for the rational observer. The difference between us, humans, and our sophisticated machines will be precisely our ability to choose life against all evidence or to imagine new life despite all past streams of bleak data. The stories in this book are all different, and yet they exude life, with its bitter and sweet taste. The economy of data, performance, and success has no meaning without an economy of life at the very heart of what we do and who we are. We will lose it all, as Professor Valentini says, if we only look at data. Action by itself is pure nonsense without an incommensurate love for life. Tangible incentives and returns are not enough to make us change. Love moves us and powers our most intimate decisions. Love for life will ignite action and will ultimately save us.

'Radical' means it all starts with me

The forty-five wonder women of this book open up completely and candidly about their journeys. It's my turn. I have not, very clearly, done enough in my life for a broader cause, and I have fully enjoyed the privilege of having been born in the right part of the planet while reaping the benefits of a good mix of luck, education, and peer pressure at work. This book is for me, personally and professionally, a starting point, which I hope will lead to a rich record of action and love for life. This is my wish for the reader. I was raised by a single mother and was always treated as a human being en route toward new and amazing horizons, despite making plenty of mistakes along the way. It's time to steal with pride from the woman who made me who I am and the women who turned this book into a spark for action and love for life. What strikes me is not their achievements, as grand and impactful as they are. These stories are relevant not only because they celebrate the 'work' to save the planet – which is much needed today – but also and especially because they restore life's wonder and richness despite its pain, limitations, and imperfections. This sense of wonder is the precondition to believe. This is exactly what's radical about it. Let's say it: it's going to be a bumpy road. We cannot be naive about what lies ahead of us. Commitment beats alignment and clarity, and that leads to action, every single day. We will disagree and struggle, more often than we like. Commitment will need to be rooted in our love for life if we care to overcome all obstacles. The message of this book is simple: love, therefore act. Let's start.

1 Paving the way

Adela Villanueva[*]

It all began with a deep sense of purpose and an unwavering belief that I could make a positive difference. I strongly believe that every individual has a role to play in creating a better world, and I was determined to play my part.

My journey started with small steps: adopting a vegan lifestyle, composting, biking, and walking, supporting circular economy practices, and advocating for other sustainable practices around me. As my passion grew, I became more involved in advocacy work and started collaborating with like-minded individuals and organizations. I began to see the power of collective action and the potential for creating lasting change.

I tried to combine that purpose with my passion for new technologies, neurosciences, moon-shot initiatives, space exploration, open innovation, biomimicry, regenerative business models, and purpose-driven and human-centered innovation. I realized that those interests, my curiosity, creativity, knowledge, and willingness to explore new ideas (and make them actionable) were my gifts to help improve the state of the world. Thanks to my open-mindedness and willingness to experiment, I have been able to explore solutions that have helped move organizations and people in the right direction.

A polyvalent approach

For more than seventeen years, I have dedicated my time and resources to responsible growth through innovation, investments, and systemic change. In my profession, I have a visionary, forward-thinking approach that supports these objectives, combining technology, open collaboration, conscious

---

[*] Entrepreneur, Impact Investor & Board Member

approaches, and new ways of deploying capital. Only in this way can we transform the world for the better.

One of my proudest achievements has been the impact I have had on various organizations that I have built, transformed, and scaled. I have helped companies become more purpose-driven, human- and planet-centered, environmentally responsible, and socially conscious. I have shown that businesses can create positive change while still being profitable, paving the way for others to follow.

One practical example is my work as a founder of Alkelio. Through this platform, we have created a space for companies and start-ups to find each other and to collaborate and innovate together, unlocking hidden opportunities that may have otherwise gone unnoticed. I believe that by working together we can achieve more significant impact than we ever could alone.

Another practical example is my work as a co-founder of the Impact Office. Through this platform, we help family offices deploy capital for good and provide collective unity to achieve a truly positive impact. We empower these offices to think more consciously about their investments, demonstrating that it's possible to create positive change while still generating returns. My work with the Impact Office is a powerful testament to my commitment to creating a world that works for everyone.

Another example is Baowa, a collective of people that I started with the shared purpose of raising collective consciousness. Through our work we hope to inspire people, wherever they are or whatever industry they work in, to think differently about their role in the world and encourage them to connect as one. By the way, Baowa means 'be at one with all.'

I am also an advocate for the principles of Burning Man as a means of changing mindsets and accelerating systemic change. I recognize that the old ways of thinking and interacting with each other and the planet are no longer sufficient to address the complex challenges we face today, and I hope that by showing a great example of co-living respectfully we can lead the charge in creating new ways of thinking that are more collaborative, inclusive, and regenerative.

Moreover, my commitment to women's empowerment, human rights, animal welfare, biodiversity preservation, and regenerative development shows my deep compassion for all living beings. We must work together if we want to create a more just and sustainable world, recognizing that we are all interconnected – and that our actions have a ripple effect on the world around us. As humans, we need to work in symbiosis with nature – and, why not, tech – to ensure a sustainable future for all.

Throughout my journey, I have learned that every action counts, no matter how small it may seem. I have learned that there are many ways to *make* change, and that we can all make a difference. It all starts with a deep sense of purpose and the willingness to act.

Remember, we all have a role to play. What is *yours*?

I hope my story inspires you to join me on this journey toward creating a more just, sustainable, and regenerative future. Together, we can thrive.

2 Tilting at windmills

Alexandra Pelka[*]

In our lives, it can be all too easy to rush headlong into new ventures. How often do we slow down and ask ourselves *where* we are or *how* we got here? It can be all too easy to forget the things that are already at our feet.

In this chapter, I want to ask these questions, making the case for the 'here' and the 'how.' These are questions that can only be answered with three essential things: time, dedication, and passion. So, let's begin.

When I first started working in sustainability, I was captivated by the allure of storytelling, of sharp communication strategies and glossy images of the fashion industry's biggest players. I was drawn in, and I thought that they must have it all figured out. But then I began to work more closely with supply chains, and I saw the severity of the challenges that face our planet. My feelings shifted between helplessness and resentment. Fortunately, I had mentors who were on hand to guide me, channeling my feelings into the possibility of action – toward justice.

Even then, I didn't figure things out right away. Growth isn't always pretty, and it's easy to feel like you're tilting at windmills, that you're knocking on doors that refuse to open. But it's important to persevere, and there will come moments – often highly surreal moments – where everything falls into place. Suddenly, you can see that you really *are* making a difference. Time, dedication, and passion – they begin to pay off.

Today, I am an internationally recognized ESG (environment, social, and corporate governance) consultant. In my work, I help companies to implement sustainability strategies – from the first to the 'last' steps. This is about implementation, communication, and transparency, and my goal is to make change happen, to foster a culture that truly embraces sustainability, and to create reporting that lets validated data speak for itself.

---

[*] ESG & SDG Consultant

Tree planters, birds, and butterflies

When I enter a company, I start with a key foundation: belief. It's a small thing with big implications. From the beginning, I set out to get a feel for the mindset of a company, asking: *how do they envision sustainability?* For some, it's seen as a virtuous asset that can drive brand awareness. You're asked to identify projects that sell well and scream, in big, green letters, *WE ARE SUSTAINABLE.* I call these companies 'the tree planters.' They think that sustainability involves planting trees and recycling PET (plastic) bottles. While these things have their place, they don't, alone, go far or deep enough.

I call the next type of companies 'the birds.' The birds think sustainability is somewhat important and know it stems from an interrelationship between different pillars – the environmental, the social, the economic. But the birds fly from one project to another – placing cookies in the cafeteria, organizing yoga classes for employees, setting up talks about mindfulness. Environmental sustainability is usually approached in a similar way to 'the tree planters,' but there is a real desire to improve.

Finally, we have 'the butterfly.' The butterfly has done the research, knows that data and validation processes are key for transformation, and is aware that things take time. The butterfly quietly begins to align departments, work groups, and suppliers. They create a growing pool of communications and data. At the end, the butterfly breaks out of its cocoon and shows everyone what they've been working on.

All three examples are positive in their own way. They all begin with first steps, and they all want to make changes and to see improvement. They're willing to reach out and seek help to improve.

As a sustainability consultant, I have dedicated my career to advocating for a healthy, balanced relationship between humanity and our planet. This connection to the environment goes beyond mere professional commitment; it is a deeply rooted commitment to and understanding of the interconnectedness of all life forms.

It was with this in mind that, in 2019, I joined the UNECE Supply Chain Transparency and Traceability Project, which focuses on a standardized way of collecting and communicating information along value chains and improving the validity of ESG reports. It's based on transparency and traceability. I help companies understand their supply chains, monitor the risks and opportunities of their environmental and social impacts, and guide them toward more conscious and sustainable business operations.

One of the main reasons I am so passionate about sustainability is my awareness of the interdependence of everything around us. Our planet is a complex web of interactions, where every action has consequences that affect the entire ecosystem. We live in a world that pivots on a delicate balance of resources, habitats, and ecosystems that allow us to live and thrive – but only if we show them the right level of respect.

I'm driven by a sense of responsibility toward our fragile world. Over time, I have learned that the balance of the earth's ecosystems also hinges on an economic perspective: companies are often only motivated to care for the planet if they can make a profit from it. This is a factor that I must absolutely take into mind. But I believe that we can indeed shift this paradigm.

When working with companies, organizations, and institutions, I take into consideration the three pillars of sustainability, working to inspire individuals, communities, and businesses to adopt sustainable practices. By instilling sustainable values across society and its actors, we can empower future generations with the knowledge, skills, and mindset to make a genuine difference. I've carried this belief for my entire life, having been brought up by parents who always encouraged me to challenge the status quo, to challenge what seems rock solid, and to seek alternative answers to those that are generally accepted.

Finding *new* answers

Before I started my career in sustainability, I studied to become a teacher. I was fascinated by the idea of passing on knowledge and by the passion we can find in questioning things that we don't feel are 'right.'

This love of education, of facilitating change and personal growth, remains with me today and continues to be an important part of my work. I still teach in my own unique way, passing on what I have learned to companies, start-ups, universities, and schools. At the heart of this is the knowledge that caring for the environment and human rights goes beyond individual efforts; it requires collective action.

In this way, I like to think of myself as more of a teacher than a consultant, communicating what I have learned while continuing to absorb new knowledge. The work we do in sustainability requires a truly open mind. But, like any educational context, it also requires collaboration and connection. When we work together, we can effect real and meaningful change.

As a sustainability and ESG expert, I help companies communicate with their suppliers in a new and deeper way. This requires a dense flow of information, all of which is used to produce reports and assessments that reflect reality – rather than a concoction of fairy tales. It's about making commitments and sharing achievements, all of it verified by real-world data. Sometimes, these reports can make for tough reading, showing the bad as well as the good. A truthful reflection of a company's performance is the bedrock of change. It goes beyond a single location, reaching across borders and continents. It encompasses entire supply chains that wrap around the world.

In a world where the challenges facing us loom large, collaboration and collective action have become catalysts for transformative movements. Coming from a fashion perspective, I like to think of it as a beautifully embroidered dress with different colored threads. Each of these threads represents a unique perspective, a cluster of expertise, a passion for collaboration. Each thread is part of a supply chain that has, until now, been hidden in the dark. Only now is it ready to step into the light.

It is not always easy to win people over to the idea of collective knowledge and collaboration. In the past, we have run our businesses in a solitary way. Sharing was associated with feeling vulnerable, fearing negative consequences, losing out. It takes time and patience to make meaningful changes. It requires that we work, passionately, together.

Early in my career, when I worked with a person who later became not only my mentor but a lifelong friend, I experienced this feeling for the first time.

On one memorable occasion, he brought an entire supply chain into a meeting room and discussed how to improve structures and processes, demonstrating how it was possible to create a strong communication protocol. There was skepticism at first. But, by the end, a plan had begun to emerge, one that would be unique and lasting. From that day forward, collaboration has been something of a personal credo for me, a conviction. That's because it is only through collaboration that companies can make real, meaningful change in their supply chains, reduce carbon emissions, and restore our precious ecosystems.

In a world that encourages individual success and competition, collaboration is the only way to create a transparent and healthy business model. I learned this lesson very quickly. That's why I foster collaborations and partnerships as much as possible and have created a global network that works across sectors to create a better future for us all.

We have seen that sustainability goes beyond the environment and that collaboration is the glue that holds all our efforts together. I have shared some insights into my career – with all its inconsistencies. I have expressed just how important knowledge and passion are in the work I do.

Reflecting on my journey, I am filled with gratitude for the mentors who have shaped my beliefs and experiences without imposing their own on me. But this journey has only just begun, and I cannot wait to write the next chapters.

I can only urge you to be aware of your own growth and to look for mentors. Surround yourself with people with whom you resonate. And while you do not have to have the same ideas or visions, be open, listen deeply, reflect, and question. You may learn something new. You may disagree completely or doubt your previous beliefs. But you will undoubtedly grow.

Remember that the power to create a more sustainable world lies in three simple mantras: be open to listening, speak the truth, and be kind in your actions. By setting a good example, you will have the power to inspire the people around you. And who knows, you may well become a mentor for another future leader. You may get to pass on all the knowledge you have accumulated and the lessons you have learned.

3   Every drop makes a difference

Antonina Sorci[*]

If I trace a line between my professional and personal life, a pattern in shades of green starts to appear. There wasn't a single moment that marked the start of my relationship with sustainability; it started on my family's farm in Sicily. It was there that I developed a sensitivity to nature and its cycles and made a silent commitment to protect it. Later in life this led me into environmental engineering and my first job in the energy sector, engaged in the energy transition.

Here, I worked on the measurement and mitigation of the impacts associated with renewable energy power plants, which ranged from innovating solutions to responding to stakeholders' growing environmental awareness. I dedicated myself to corporate sustainability issues in the round, supporting the origination and implementation of sustainable development projects and initiatives at both business division and cross-divisional level.

In 2019, as a volunteer technician, I took part in a mission to Laos with the NGO Elettrici Senza Frontiere (Electricians without Borders). They focus on developing and implementing livelihoods projects in places that lack or have minimal access to the electricity grid. I contributed to a sustainable electrification project with the Aka, an ancient ethnic group that lives in the deep north of the country. This involved installing photovoltaic systems in several villages, so they can now benefit from a brighter and more comfortable environment. During the month I was there, I shared the small rural dwellings in the Aka community. This out-of-the-ordinary experience enriched my understanding of sustainability and raised my awareness of how the perfect but delicate balance between humans and nature that characterizes places such as the Aka villages is threatened by climate change.

---

[*] Sustainability Project Leader & Co-founder, Upgreene

My time to act

Later, in 2022, I co-founded Upgreene, a start-up that focuses on measuring, offsetting, and tracking the carbon footprint associated with products and services using blockchain technology. By taking a 'sustainability as a service' approach, we aim to bring small and medium-sized enterprises closer to ESG (environment, social, and corporate governance) issues in a way that considers their value chain peculiarities and is grounded in robust science.

Through this initiative, my early commitment to protect the planet was realized. I decided to devote my time to measuring the CO_2 emissions associated with production processes. Accurate measurement is an essential step to understanding impact and helps to set the baseline for embarking on a path of improvement based on targets to reduce emissions. As noted in the World Economic Forum's latest *Global Risk Report*, climate change is the main threat we will face in the next decade. We are reminded of this every day as we witness more frequent extreme weather events such as droughts and wildfires. The data shows that the average temperature worldwide during the twentieth century increased by 1.1°C. Weather analysis stretching back to 1880 tells us that we are experiencing the hottest temperatures on record, with 2020 in first position, followed by 2016, then 2019, 2015, 2017, 2021, 2018, and 2014.

The scientific community now unanimously recognizes human activities and associated atmospheric emissions as the primary cause of this exceptional global warming. Studies show an almost linear relationship between cumulative anthropogenic CO_2 emissions and global warming: for every 1,000 Gigatons of CO_2 of cumulative emissions, the global surface temperature rises by about 0.45°C.

The Paris Agreement is the reference target for all climate plans at national and continental level, including the European Green Deal. The agreement has been signed by 197 countries and commits to limit the temperature increase to "well below 2°C" and preferably to 1.5°C compared with pre-industrial levels. To limit warming to 1.5°C, emissions will have to be reduced by 45% globally already by 2030, and net zero will have to be reached by 2050, which means that we must stay within a so-called available carbon budget.

In this context, deep decarbonization of value chains (Scope 1, 2, and 3) should be the top priority for companies, along with investment in high-quality carbon credits to offset unabated emissions year after year. Thanks also to pressure from consumers and investors, many companies have been driven to act on climate change and have set ambitious targets to reduce their carbon footprint.

The issues of carbon footprint measurement and transition planning toward carbon neutrality by 2050 are also covered in new European directives, the Due Diligence in Corporate Sustainability Directive, and the Corporate Sustainability Reporting Directive. This means that in general, companies will be required to provide much more transparent, complete, and accurate information to the market on governance, strategies, risk assessment, metrics, and corporate objectives on climate change. It also introduces the concept of Double Materiality, which requires that impact analysis is performed from two angles: 'inside-out,' to understand how the company's activities impact the environment and people through products and/or services; and 'outside-in,' to show how sustainability risks and opportunities affect or may affect the company's cash flows, development, performance, positioning, cost of capital, or access to finance in the short, medium, or long term.

These regulatory changes pose new reporting challenges for companies. I strongly believe in the importance of change enablers that support these companies to navigate through this uncharted territory and help them to seize the opportunities they encounter on the journey, for example strengthening their relationships with their stakeholders or their role as a responsible actor in sustainable development.

Climate change is an amplifier of existing problems, including poverty and poor health; limited availability of water, food, and energy; and loss of biodiversity. Thus, acting to reduce and mitigate climate impacts helps companies contribute to the sustainable development goals. This is my small contribution to trying to bring about change; it's just a small drop in the ocean, but every drop makes a difference.

4   Empowering women to ignite global change

*Bianca Bonetti**

Have you ever met a teenager who *doesn't* want to spend their summer on the beach? Well, I'm one of them. That's because I'm in love with glaciers, with mountain tops and snow-bound hillsides. I used to beg my parents to send me to summer ski courses all year round, disavowing the sea in favor of the slopes.

Over the years, I have made close friends with the slopes and the stones that poke their faces from the blankets of white. I have fallen in love with the sun burning my face, the scent of pine, and the harshness of the wind. But above all, I have made friends with the colors of the glaciers – with the icy, unexpected blues that you only ever see at the very heights of the mountains. Here, you can sense the ancient history of the hills, of landmarks that feel like they have been here forever.

But every year, those same mountains and hills – which once felt so ancient – seem ever more fragile. Today, I fear that they are on the cusp of disappearing.

All those years of skiing and snow have allowed me to witness the vagaries of climate change with my very own eyes. In years past, however, there was little talk about things such as sustainability and climate change. All I had to go on were the stones and the rocks, a little more exposed each season. If you don't believe me, there is a beautiful experiment you can do for yourself. Go and visit the Morteratsch glacier in Switzerland. Over the past century, this natural monument has retreated well over two kilometers. People will tell you how they can visualize this retreat: "In 1990, the glacier was here." "In 1995, the glacier was here." On it goes.

But why worry about all this chilly ice and snow? For many, the slopes are the source of their water supply. As Alejandra Borunda of National Geo-

---

* Founder Girls Went Out & Sisters Founders

graphic observes: "The high mountains cradle more ice and snow on their peaks than exists anywhere else on the planet besides the poles. More than 200,000 glaciers, snowdrifts, high-altitude lakes, and wetlands: together, the high mountains contain about half of all the freshwater used by humans." These glaciers – these hillsides and mountains – are not just winter playgrounds. They are the lifeblood of our planet. They water us. They hydrate us. They are the wellspring of our planet.

Awareness-raising

I had a very principled upbringing. We always recycled at home and got in big trouble if we forgot. We didn't eat meat. Nor did we take planes. This lifestyle feels positively avant-garde now. In the end, you are what you learn. And I grew up learning a great respect for nature.

These statements are easy to make. They can sound like platitudes. But I have seen first-hand the detrimental effects of not sufficiently caring. I have seen these things with my own eyes. I have seen the sacred cows of India eat plastic left on the streets. I have seen people throwing snack wrappers from the windows of cars. I have walked streets where you can't find a place to dispose of rubbish. I have been on beaches where idly buried refuse is returned by the swells of the ocean.

It was while traveling that I discovered that the world was quickly becoming one big rubbish heap. We, in the 'developed' West, are often spared this realization, keeping our countries 'beautiful' while selling our waste to those in the global South. I still remember the stench of Cairo's Garbage City, home to over 250,000 people.

But it wasn't until 2014 that I had my great epiphany. Moving to Argentina for a year, I lived in a neighborhood in the south of Cordoba. During my years in Switzerland, I had always taken a tram to travel to university. Here, I would take a taxi, the car making its winding way past vast favelas. Looking upon all this poverty, I asked myself: *How can we make these people's lives better? How can we offer them a better lifestyle, a better quality of life?*

In *Factfulness*, Hans Rosling answers many of these questions. In the process, he debunks many of the fallacies that divide the world into binaries of 'rich vs. poor' and 'developed vs. undeveloped.' Ultimately, he emphasizes the existence of a highly differentiated group of middle-class countries in which most of the world's population resides. And he puts us on the alert. Asia, he observes, is 'entering' the middle class. This offers the opportunity of significant economic development, but he warns that this should be accompanied by increased education on sustainability – that there is an opportunity, now, to 'leapfrog' our reliance on fossil fuels.

For many emerging markets and 'middle-class' countries, there is immense potential to drive sustainable change and economic growth. I agree with Rosling. I agree that, by shifting our perspective and focusing our attention on these 'new' and emerging markets, we can unlock a wealth of innovative ideas and new solutions. And the role of entrepreneurs *in* this future will be key.

Entrepreneurship: A catalyst for change across borders

In our Eurocentric world, it's vital that real change come from emerging markets, whose economies are home to some 80% of the world's population. These centers are the engine of global population growth, and their share of global GDP rises in tandem with their populations, and particularly with their middle class. Indeed, these regions offer unique and often overlooked perspectives and opportunities. Guided by this thought, and to make a tangible impact, I made the decision several years ago to move to Africa, dedicating three years of my life to helping young entrepreneurs partner with local governments to launch their own sustainable businesses. Observing the untapped potential, talent, and determination of these entrepreneurs, I became convinced that change can indeed be initiated at the grassroots level, and that this is the only way to act.

What I call 'leapfrogging' will play an essential role in this process. In Europe, we moved from coins and cash to checks, and eventually to bank accounts. These banks, these institutions, are highly regulated. In Kenya, meanwhile, society has moved from cash to the sending of money via SMS – almost like phone credit. But what does this have to do with sustainability? A lot. As with the case of SMS money transfers, I believe that it's entirely possible for emerging markets to 'leapfrog' the old ways and to embrace the new, immediately adopting advanced technologies and alternative energy sources – skipping the oh-so-European dependence on fossil fuels.

In recent years, I have done a lot of work in energy and agricultural development. Both fields have much to do with education. And it's precisely in countries most at risk to the vagaries of climate change that young entrepreneurs are most attentive to the effect of their businesses on local communities. This isn't something we could necessarily say of our 'developed' world. Events such as the Covid-19 pandemic have helped us see how interconnected the global system really is. "Look," we said, "how things on the other side of the world have implications for us at home." While I have left Africa behind, my years there taught me the value of networks and networking. I learned the power of innovation and resilience.

Women as agents of transformation

While living for many years between Egypt, Côte d'Ivoire, and Tanzania, my greatest discovery was the role played by women's communities in shaping a sustainable future. Why? Because women have a unique perspective, one of respect, empathy, and collaborative strength. When they, when *we*, work together, I see something silent and magical. It was with this in mind that, during the dark days of Covid-19, I started Girls Went Out – a platform designed to empower women through outdoor sports. In 2022, in the aftermath of the pandemic, I launched Community Sisters Founders – a community of Italian-speaking female entrepreneurs. Taken together, these projects reflect my lifelong goal to provide networks and resources that amplify women's voices, to catalyze real and meaningful change in the world that we share. Indeed, I dream of a world where women – all women – have equal opportunities, where they can all enjoy education, political power, and professional opportunities. After all, women create life. They embody an innate, global power – and this is the root of my respect for them, for *us*. I see this power reflected in the fact that, statistically, women's businesses are more likely to be focused on social and environmental impacts. Women seek to give back.

And this giving back won't happen without communication, without raising awareness.

I work as a speakers' manager for a company that organizes innovation events. It's a job that allows me to promote ideas that educate and engage the world about the urgency of climate change. And the needle is shifting. Each year, in October, we organize a flagship event in Zurich, bringing together experts, thought leaders, and change advocates, all of whom are dedicated to innovation and collaboration. As a global leader in sustainability, Switzerland provides the ideal backdrop for this event. And the need couldn't be more pressing, nor more self-evident. 2022 saw the first winter in which European ski slopes had to close due to a lack of snow. Such events, as 'minor' as they might seem, gesture toward the pressurized global scenario we find ourselves in. I hope that future generations can ski all summer long, like I used to do. I wish them a bountiful, healthy planet. I wish them a future. And that future is within our reach.

5 Investing in the future

Cassandra Harris[*]

After starting my career in media with advertising giants WPP GroupM, Mindshare, and Mediacom, I transitioned into the venture space. Drawing on the experience I gained working with Fortune 500 companies and within multinational agencies, I founded Venturespring, one of London's first corporate venture studios, focused on building, launching, and accelerating ventures on behalf of large blue-chips such as Vodafone, Tata Communications, and Coca-Cola.

In 2017, one of our accelerator programs was set to send start-ups to Sir Richard Branson's Necker Island as a prize. But just as we launched this initiative, Hurricane Irma struck the island, making it impossible to send the founders there. We improvised by sending them to Branson's Verbier lodge instead; however, this incident marked a turning point in my career. I realized that I needed to shift my energy and focus on businesses that help fight climate change and other global challenges.

A different type of VC

My route into VC was unconventional. Although I studied business at university, which included finance, I didn't major in the subject and chose computers and marketing instead. I joined the sector twelve years ago when I was asked to help build a very early-stage venture fund as part of another start-up I co-founded. Despite having no equity or carry in the fund, learning and applying the venture fund formation process was a crucial step in my career journey.

A venture studio isn't the most scalable business to run, and scalability is key to addressing problems at a global scale – so I started to think about

---

[*] Serial Entrepreneur, Investor & TV Series Producer

how to build an 'automated conveyor belt' platform to fund and accelerate pre-existing ventures rather than building them from scratch in my
studio. This thought evolved and eventually led to the formation of my
newest business, Litestream, which I've strategically kept under wraps
while we ramp up our infrastructure and operational processes.

Building an ecosystem

Litestream's mission is to partner with some of the world's largest venture
funds to build the world's most scalable platform to discover, invest in, and
scale ESG (environment, social, and corporate governance)-driven ventures
using the power of media. Through strategic media partnerships, we promote impact-driven start-ups within their portfolios while also identifying
and directing their capital toward other promising ventures that align with
our missions. My goal is to bring together a powerful community and create
a platform to accelerate visionary founders and their disruptive technologies
to help drive positive change and improve the lives of one billion people.
At the heart of this mission sits the idea of making wealth accessible to all
while making a positive impact on humanity.

Noting how the early stages of the Covid-19 pandemic caused VC funding to decrease by almost 30% and created a ripple of knock-on effects that
have yet to subside, I knew I needed to stay ahead of the curve. With this in
mind, I stepped away from the traditional fund model (primarily due to the
lack of revenue streams and the inherently challenging nature of building a
first-time fund) and focused instead on creating a diverse and international
community of co-investors including Buoyant Ventures, Una Terra Ventures, Burnt Island Ventures, Agfunder, Prelude Ventures, and others with
similar missions.

We have also been building a unique plug-and-play technology that facil-
itates real-time interactivity, allowing viewers to invest in or purchase from
the featured start-ups on our platform. It also partners with media properties
to create regionally focused communities of millions of users and viewers
whose direct input supports and promotes the ventures that the company
highlights and holds equity positions in. Unlike on or offline accelerators,
crowdfunding platforms, or marketing engines, Litestream offers an all-
in-one solution, enabling start-ups and growth-stage companies to attract
investors and expand their customer base simultaneously. By endorsing investors and companies that seek to address the world's most urgent environmental and social challenges, we aim to make a genuine impact in the world.

Investing in ventures that focus on issues such as climate change and
biodiversity loss can make a significant positive impact on the world. By

supporting these ventures, we can help drive innovation and encourage the development of sustainable solutions. Not only do these ventures have the potential to create a better future for people and the planet, but they can also provide financial returns for investors. Impact-driven start-ups have shown strong growth potential, with studies indicating that sustainable companies outperform their traditional counterparts in the long run.

Investing in sustainable ventures and leveraging the power of strategic media partnerships to promote them is a powerful way to support positive change and drive progress toward a more sustainable future. It is not only an opportunity to make a positive impact on the world but also a wise investment decision for those looking for long-term financial returns.

But investors and businesses are only one part of the puzzle. To reach our ambitious goals, we are working to build an ecosystem of climate activists, social impact entrepreneurs, media and entertainment professionals, distributors, influencers, and celebrity talent – all galvanized around the same mission.

Technology has the potential to help solve some of the world's biggest problems. That's why investing in the right solutions and accelerating them as much as possible is of crucial importance – this is a point that I emphasize repeatedly. The environment will remain my major focus, but what's even more inspiring is the fact that climate change is, no pun intended, just the tip of the iceberg. Gender equality, global health, access to clean, affordable energy, poverty, and even loneliness are all issues that can be tackled by this generation's passionate innovators and lateral thinkers – and I can't wait to see how the next few years unfold.

Whether you're a founder, an investor, or just energized by the possibility of a brighter future, the time to act is now, and I invite you wholeheartedly to join us and become part of the solution.

6   The urgency of sustainable action

*Catalina Valentino**

I spent a long time thinking about what to write for this chapter, deciding – ultimately – to focus on *action*. I'm hoping to inspire you to get up, to get out there, and to make a difference – even if that means you ditch the rest of this chapter, slam the book shut, and hit the streets. It's time to step up and be the heroine this world needs. So, let's get started.

Sustainability

Sustainability is not just a trendy buzzword; it is a necessity for our planet's survival. We live in a world that faces multiple environmental crises, from climate change to loss of biodiversity, and change is urgently needed. It is not enough to simply talk about the importance of sustainability. We must act on it.

But this isn't new information. The good news is that action is within our reach, and by taking simple steps in our daily lives we *can* make a real difference.

To begin, consider changing your viewpoint. Take a moment to reflect on someone important to you. What do they resemble, and what emotions do they evoke in you? Next, contemplate a scenario in which this person no longer existed. Soon, we may face a world that is unsuitable for human habitation, both socially and environmentally. So, the person who came to mind earlier? Reach out and take action to secure their future as well as your own in this world.

Abu Dhabi

Now, picture the future for a moment as I begin to tell the story of a woman I met in Abu Dhabi. It was a night I will always cherish. The stars

---

* CEO & Co-founder, Elixr

were visible, the desert breeze balanced out the heat, and I had just left
The Forbes Women 30/50 desert closing party. During the event, I had
the privilege of meeting and networking with inspiring women from all
over the world, including Hillary Clinton, Olena Volodymyrivna Zelens-
ka, Gloria Steinem, Catherine O'Hara, Jessica Alba, Billie Jean King, and
more. It had been a full three days of intense workshops, insightful panel
discussions, and engaging conversations. I was feeling exhausted – but
fulfilled.

As I stepped outside the venue, I realized that taxis were infrequent in
this part of the desert, and I might have to wait a while to catch a ride back
to my hotel. I waited for the best part of an hour until I was approached
by a smiling man in a golf cart who offered to take me 500 meters to the
nearest pick-up spot. There was a taxi waiting and, to my pleasant surprise,
the driver was a woman. I blurted out my shock at the rarity of such a sight
in the United Arab Emirates. She beamed with joy and thanked me. Her
exuberance was infectious, and I couldn't help but smile. "Woohooo," she
shouted, chuckling away as she sped up.

As we drove, she showed a keen interest in my life and was genuinely
inspired by my accomplishments, excited by the idea of a young half-Co-
lombian female running multiple companies. Little did she know I would
be the one taking the most inspiration away that night.

During the drive, she opened up to me, sharing the struggle of having
to leave her children back home with her mother to come and work in Abu
Dhabi after her husband died. She would stop to reflect for a moment, but
her happiness was contagious. It radiated from her like the warm glow of
the Abu Dhabi sun, and it was impossible not to be swept up in it. I had
never seen anyone so at peace with their life. It was truly a beautiful encounter, and one that moved me in a way that I can't find the words for.

As she told me about her life in Abu Dhabi, I was struck by the beauty
of her soul. It was a reminder of just how fortunate most of us are, and how
often we take our privileges for granted. This amazing woman had so little,
and yet she was so full of joy and gratitude. At that moment, I knew that I
had to do something to help her. I withdrew a substantial amount of cash
and handed it to her, hoping to make a difference in her life. It was a small
gesture, but it meant the world to her.

It was a beautiful moment, one that will stay with me forever. And it inspired me to do something bigger, and more meaningful. I realized that we
all have the power to make a difference in the world, no matter how small
our actions may seem. Sustainability is about more than just the environment. It's about making a positive impact on society and the economy. At
that moment, I knew that I had done just that. I had made a positive impact

on this wonderful, resilient woman and had been served a reminder that every action we make sends ripples beyond what we can see.

So don't be discouraged by the size of your actions. Even the smallest gestures can have a huge impact on someone's life. And who knows, maybe that act of kindness will inspire them to pay it forward and create a chain reaction of positivity and change. That beautiful night in Abu Dhabi was a reminder of the power of compassion, and it inspired me to continue to do my part in creating a better world for all.

Action

As I trailed back to my hotel room, I started thinking about what I could do to make a difference. Cash is great, but we also need to focus on reducing inequalities and quality education, to support decent work and economic growth. I knew I wanted to create a lasting impact, and so, on that mild night in Abu Dhabi, the seed was planted for the idea that would become the Elixr Foundation. Through this foundation, my co-founders and I address climate and social issues through the art of storytelling to align with the Sustainable Development Goals, cultivating social, economic, and environmental balance in the process.

My co-founder Joseph Michael Daniels deployed the first-ever connected net zero building technology across four continents before playing pivotal roles in policy for BEIS (the UK's Department for Business, Energy & Industrial Strategy) and the UKBCSD (UK Business Council for Sustainable Development). Together, we built the sustainable tech venture builder Elixr, and we now have eight major sustainable tech ventures of the future in our portfolio, focusing on making every one of those ready for market this year. We structured our organization in a way that not only supports sustainable companies but also channels profits to charities and the foundation, enabling us to do good work. We can all strive to implement ESG (environment, social, and corporate governance) strategies in our organizations.

So, how can we begin to tackle these issues? Let's start by looking at the big picture. According to the IPCC, there is a greater than 50% probability that the global temperature increase will reach or exceed 1.5°C by 2040, based on analysis of multiple scenarios.

However, under a high-emissions pathway, the world may surpass this threshold even earlier, between 2018 and 2037. The urgency of the need to take action to reduce GHG emissions is clear, as the consequences of exceeding this temperature limit would be devastating for our planet and all its inhabitants.

To limit global warming, the United Nations has called for a 45% reduction in global GHG emissions by 2030, with the goal of reaching net zero emissions by 2050. While this represents a daunting challenge, it is an achievable goal if we collaborate and act collectively. Failing to meet this target would result in irreversible damage to our planet and its ecosystems, making it imperative that we work together to reduce our carbon footprint and transition to a sustainable future.

Many people may feel overwhelmed by the prospect of changing their life-styles. However, it is important to note that the primary message is to reduce the amount of carbon emissions generated by our daily activities. These facts don't demand perfection, but rather a collective effort to be better. And there are a few immediate actions that, on scale, could make a huge difference.

A recent study by the University of Oxford found that if everyone in the UK switched to a plant-based diet, it could reduce GHG emissions by 8%.

According to the World Bank, global waste is expected to increase by 70% by 2050. We can all do our part by recycling, composting, and reducing our use of single-use plastics. While I can understand the convenience and hygiene factor of single-use plastics, what's the point of using a product for a few minutes that will then take hundreds of years to decompose? It's like buying a disposable car for a quick trip to the grocery store. So, unless you're planning on preserving your plastic spoon in a time capsule for future generations to marvel at, it's time to ditch the disposable plastics and opt for more sustainable alternatives.

We can make a difference

As I mentioned earlier in this chapter, now is the time for action. Climate change affects all of us, but it disproportionately affects the most vulnerable communities, such as those living in poverty or in areas prone to natural disasters. These people have no power to do anything about it. *But we do.* And while we like to feel good about ourselves and forget about things that make us feel uncomfortable, it's time to shift this mindset. Because of our better fortune, it is our responsibility to speak for those who can't.

By acting on sustainability, we can help to reduce these inequalities and ensure a better future for everyone. It's a critical issue that requires urgent action, and we cannot afford to wait for others to take the lead; we must each do our part in our daily lives and in our communities. By reducing our carbon footprint, reducing waste, leading social justice, and promoting sustainable business practices, we can create a better future for ourselves and for future generations. The power of action is within our grasp. Let's use it to make a difference.

7   Something extraordinary in a world of normal

Christina Senn-Jakobsen[*]

I was born into a world of 'normal.' Growing up in a small town in Denmark, I lived in an ordinary house with fruit trees, a big vegetable garden, happily married parents, a brother, and a dog. We cooked our meals at home. We purchased food according to a strict budget, only supplementing the things we grew for ourselves. Shared meals were the tasty social glue that held our day-to-day lives together. Life was good – albeit rather uneventful.

The environment and our impact on the wider world, beyond our happy little bubble, wasn't really on our radar. The only time I used the word 'climate' was when referring to our car's air conditioning system. I didn't know anyone who would choose *not* to eat meat and certainly couldn't fathom why someone would only eat plants. My biggest 'crisis' was choosing what to wear as a teenager.

Today, my relationship with food is just as complex as the global systems that produce it. I remain a true lover of food. But the carefree bubble of my childhood has most definitely burst. When I sink my teeth into a delicious dish, I taste the entire value chain that brought it to my plate. Wiping my mouth, I realize that food is really something extraordinary, that it involves a whole sequence of choices that we make – and that every single dish, however simple or small, has an impact on our health. But it also has an impact on the health of our planet.

As society underwent rapid industrialization and sought new ways to feed an ever-growing population, our food systems became more complex and destructive. But I know that there are people out there doing everything they can to reshape these systems into a force for good. This is what keeps me motivated.

[*] Managing Director, Swiss Food & Nutrition Valley

Finding my purpose

After studying Food Science in Copenhagen and Wageningen, I worked in the branded consumer goods industry for over twelve years. Perhaps it was my 'normal' childhood that triggered the adventurer in me. In a whirlwind of roles from Germany and Switzerland to Norway and India, I learned about product development, innovation, and how to spot emerging market opportunities. But I was still working within the system. I hadn't yet taken a step back to realize how desperately it needed to be transformed.

This journey – the one that led me to find my true purpose – began nine years ago. When I became a mother, I took time out from my corporate career. I started working with a leading accelerator to help them bridge the gap between start-ups, corporates, governments, foundations, and universities, working to accelerate deep tech innovation. I was immediately hooked.

Working alongside start-ups opened my eyes to the challenges facing our food system and the critical importance of sustainability. These creative minds and courageous teams had not just pinned down the problems. They were actively building new technologies and service models to tackle them. Having grown up with the legacy of the industrial revolution, it represented an enormous shift in perspective.

Inspired by these experiences, I co-wrote an article about uniting the Swiss food ecosystem's innovation forces under one roof. It read like a manifesto, a vision for the future that emphasized the unique density of influential players we have around us, here in Switzerland. This abundance presents both an opportunity and a responsibility in our quest to revolutionize our food system.

Then, just three years later, I received a call. Several leading Swiss food actors had come together to create the Swiss Food & Nutrition Valley, a non-profit purpose-driven association created to unite the Swiss ecosystem and unlock its innovation potential. It was just as I had described it in my article. They needed a Managing Director to drive the project forward and wondered if I was interested. And that's how I landed my dream job.

Pioneering future-proof food systems, together

Today, the Valley encompasses more than 130 partners – from multinational companies such as Nestlé, Bühler, Givaudan, and DSM-Firmenich through to leading academic institutions, accelerators, small and medium-sized enterprises, and start-ups. The strength of our ecosystem is its diversity, where each partner inside the Valley is able to leave competition at the doorstep, working, collectively, toward a common mission.

And this joint mission is powerful indeed. Together, in just three years, we have launched a series of impact platforms; developed tools to help partners access the talent, investment, and facilities they need to grow and scale; and built strong partnerships to connect Swiss innovators with opportunities across the globe. We currently have projects in the pipeline on precision nutrition, cultured foods, food waste, and controlled environmental agriculture. Ultimately, we are led by our partners. Where they see opportunities, we do our very best to connect them with the people and resources they need to drive change.

Switzerland may be a small and landlocked nation, nestled at the heart of Europe, but it has a huge food system. And we are actively building bridges with countries with complementary strengths – from the Netherlands and Denmark to Israel and Singapore. Together, we are working to accelerate our impact on the global stage, bringing the future of food closer, faster.

Small action, big impact

The more I learn about our food systems, about the actors who produce it – from field to fork – the more I feel a sense of responsibility. As a little girl, I was raised to do my best. I was taught that doing my best was always good enough, no matter the result. This mentality has been immensely helpful in my career. It means I'm not afraid of tackling big challenges.

I consider it a privilege to be able to work alongside talented and passionate change-makers from across the globe, to use our knowledge, connections, and experiences to accelerate meaningful transformations in our food system.

And these are transformations that will always come about through collective solutions. After all, small actions brought us to where we are today – with a food system that is damaging not only our climate but our physical health. But these same 'small' actions can, I believe, help us find our way out again.

The power of normal

Everyone in this book is a normal person, one whose journey just happened to expose them to a situation or challenge that helped them find their purpose. I applaud all the innovators who have made the decision to drive change as part of their daily jobs and lives.

But I also admire everyone who – while juggling being a partner, parent, and professional – takes the time to consider what they can do to make the world around them a better place. As citizens of the world, we all have the power to shape our food system through the choices we make in our every-day normal lives.

By taking the time to understand the realities of our food system, we can understand its role in protecting the world we live in. Together, we can figure out the kinds of changes that we can *all* make. It's not about striving for perfection, but about doing better. Little by little. Meal by meal. Bite by bite. This is the true power of normal. So, let's be normal together.

8   The way of 'wa'

*Christine Harada**

Harmony. In Japanese, it is written down as 和 (meaning 'wa'). Specifically, *wa* connotes harmony within a group, requiring an attitude of cooperation and a recognition of the social roles we play *within* that group. Harmony forms the foundational framework of many Japanese values. So much so, in fact, that this kanji is used to describe anything that is considered 'Japanese':

和紙 (*washi*) = Japanese paper
和歌 (*waka*) = a (classical) Japanese poem
和服 (*wafuku*) = Japanese (traditional) clothes
和風 (*wafū*) = Japanese style

It is no accident that *wa* is the oldest recorded name for Japan, occurring in several ancient Chinese texts. The Japanese also borrowed the same kanji to write the name of the Yamato kingdom from which the nation of Japan is descended. Indeed, *wa* was so important that it featured in the 7th-century CE Japanese constitution, laying a moral framework for the nation itself. *Wa* is still a big part of how the Japanese see themselves. But it's also how I see myself and the world around me.

I grew up in Los Angeles with deep roots in Japanese culture. I remember being taught that harmony is the ultimate value. There was a recognition, and constant reinforcement, that I was a part of an interdependent society. My sense of self is defined through my interactions with others and not merely through the force of my individual personality. Dependence on others is a natural and necessary part of the human condition; it is viewed negatively only when the social obligations it creates are too onerous to fulfill. My passion for the work I do in sustainability starts and ends with 和 – with *wa*.

---

* Former US Chief Sustainability Officer

Turning points

As I reflect on my life thus far, there are three turning points that led me to work on a path toward a sustainable future.

The first was as a five-year-old. I remember it clearly, looking out of a giant window at a Boeing 747, a machine that could seamlessly take my family and me to my grandparents' house in Tokyo. The 747 was enormous, filling the entire frame of the airport window, shimmering in the Los Angeles sun.

I was so excited to start the journey to Japan with my mother and sister. We were flying to Tokyo like we did every summer, just as school ended, to celebrate Obon. Obon is a summer holiday for which many people travel home to spend time with their family. The experience of being transported by this giant jet was inspiring.

As we walked down the jet bridge into the plane, we could feel the heat from the summer day. We took this flight every summer and, when I walked through the plane door, I would peer to my left and see the pilots getting ready for our flight in the cockpit. The flight attendants greeted us. They were friendly and wearing uniforms of navy and gold. They were constantly smiling, helping us to the right seats and handing my sister and me pins that resembled airplanes. I put mine on, thinking I was part of an elite club that could move people around the world. My sister sat in a window seat next to me. I would regularly peer out the window, getting glimpses of the view of the world far below us. Within a few minutes after take-off, I could see all of Los Angeles. I loved the sensation of soaring above the clouds, like a bird. It was such a miracle to me that humans could conquer the sky with such technology. Eleven hours later, I would be immersed in a land full of people who looked like me – in the urban jungle that is Tokyo.

The experience of seeing how everything is so interconnected from the airplane was incredibly inspiring. It reminded me of the oneness that we all share with the earth. It reminded me that I have a part to play, alongside millions of others, in harmony.

The second turning point came in the form of an epiphany – a gut feeling that tells you an answer that you immediately know is *right*. I was in high school, standing in line outside and waiting to buy a coke. As I waited, counting the change in my hand, I looked up and I saw a plane. I remember having a sudden moment of clarity: that I wanted to design airplanes. This led me to apply to study aerospace engineering at the Massachusetts Institute of Technology (MIT). At MIT, we learned aerospace design through a very systems-oriented curriculum called Unified Engineering – the sophomore-level engineering course taken by every undergraduate who joins the Department of Aeronautics and Astronautics.

In this course, several different engineering fields are introduced in a unified format – highlighting the systemic nature of aerospace engineering. We learned how the smallest changes to an aerospace design carry implications for the entire system. There is a tremendous benefit to covering these disciplines in such a format.

I came out of the program understanding the interaction between statics and dynamics in structures, and how fluid dynamics impact propulsion, and in turn its impact on the control systems, and more. As a result, I still tend to think in terms of systems. Systems thinking involves a sensitivity to the circular nature of the world we live in, an awareness of the role of structure in creating the conditions we face, a recognition that there are powerful laws of systems operating that we are frequently unaware of, and a realization that there are consequences of our actions to which we may be oblivious. Systems *matter*.

After earning my degree, my first job was to design, build, launch, and operate satellites – and not just one satellite, but a whole *constellation* of satellites. I was assigned to the Iridium program, a telecommunications satellite system that provided wireless mobile communications through a network of sixty-six satellites in polar, low-earth orbits. I was on the team that designed the guidance, navigation, and controls system – the subsystem that tells the satellite how it should orient itself relative to the earth, and how to adjust its orbit if needed.

Iridium was at the leading edge of the spacecraft industry at the time. Its satellites are the only ones that communicate with one another as well as bounce signals back to earth. This capability makes the system the only one in the world that can connect any two points on our planet. To give an example: Should a North Pole explorer have an immediate need to reach a South Pole colleague, they can.

Iridium is also easy to use while in motion, as finding the nearest of the sixty-six orbiting satellites requires only a small telephone antenna. Unfortunately, though, the system was planned in the mid-1980s and was already archaic by the time it was deployed in 1998. The Iridium business plan that was locked in twelve years before the system became operational did not anticipate the explosion in data services that would take place in the mid-1990s. This is where I took away the key lesson that economic viability is crucial for a solution to be successful in the long term. Plans *matter*.

The third turning point came when I was appointed Federal Chief Sustainability Officer for President Barack Obama. The US federal government is an institution like no other. Its reach is colossal, its structure complex, its workforce enormous. Difficult job? That's an understatement. But few jobs are more important. After all, I feel that there is no greater purpose in life than to serve, having the opportunity to directly influence decisions that impact the citizens of our entire nation, if not the world. This level of influence over issues that I get out of bed each day to solve is almost impossible to get anywhere else. It's exciting, and extraordinarily fulfilling. For my readers, I highly encourage each one of you to seriously consider spending some time working for the government.

The scale of the federal government's operations at the time presented a tremendous opportunity. With 320,000 buildings, 650,000 vehicles, and $445 billion annually in purchased goods and services, it was a great platform to develop and advance sustainability practices and policies, and to help agencies prepare for and respond to the impacts of climate change on their operations and services.

Beyond environmental protection, sustainability in the federal government called for a much broader view that encompasses economic transformation, political action, and – of course – business activity. I found that the most rewarding part of my work was progressing and supporting economic opportunity through the climate crisis, thinking creatively about solutions that are affordable and accessible.

Sustainability and climate change were a core platform and pillar of the Obama administration's agenda. President Obama led the charge to move forward domestically and internationally, to lead by example – to make sure that the federal government was on the forefront of climate action. We developed and launched President Obama's sustainability plan to decarbonize the federal government and ensure that this was indeed a whole-of-government effort. We developed a comprehensive suite of actions, always reminding ourselves to *implement, implement, implement*. One of the core pieces of our government work was to think through how to best organize other governments to decarbonize their operations. This led to several announcements with the governments of Canada and Mexico at the North American Leaders' Summit in 2016.

Keeping our promises

The Obama administration's policies and my work within it laid critical groundwork for the field of sustainability and addressing climate change. It is gratifying to see the explosion in the number of stakeholders from the private sector, NGOs, and governments in the years since who are pushing forward the conversation and action on climate action. I am encouraged to see the great momentum behind it, where decarbonization in the United States has proceeded apace. Many promises have been made by corporations and governments and it is critical that we continue to implement them and ensure that they are kept. Our future ambitions for decarbonization require us to raise the bar.

Walking the walk toward a net zero world requires harmony – harmony in the way we interact with one another, the way we live among our communities, and the way we live with the earth. Success can come only if we all put forth our best individual efforts – and if we work *together*. The best decisions are often made after consulting with everyone in a group and getting different perspectives so we can understand where we would fail and how we can make our solutions stronger. Consensus does not imply that there has been universal agreement, but this style of consultative decision-making involves each member of the group in an information exchange, reinforces feelings of group identity, and makes the implementation of the decision smoother – and much more enduring. I encourage all of us, in our everyday lives, to try to be a part of a harmonious future – not just for a better present day, but for a brighter tomorrow.

9   Radical change

Daniela Marmentini[*]

My path toward sustainability has not always been straight. My first love was for documentaries and photography, and this is why, on leaving high school, I studied film, pursuing a ten-year career in film and TV production.

But as the years passed, I felt the urge for some radical change. This is why I returned to university to study biology, despite the difficulty of starting over at the age of thirty. With each exam my passion grew, and my studies reconnected me with a childhood passion for the wonders of the natural world. Graduating in Environmental Biology, I had the opportunity to engage with such fascinating topics as plant physiology, ecological restoration, biodiversity, and sustainability. I had fallen in love with science.

After graduating, I had the opportunity to start working as a Sustainability Manager for Agricooltur, an innovative start-up based just outside Turin. They produce aeroponic cultivation systems that will help us to revolutionize the food production chain and our wider consumption paradigm. This gave me the chance to dive deep into the way our food is designed, and I feel very lucky to actively work every day with my colleagues toward redesigning food production in a regenerative way – helping nature and biodiversity to thrive. The food industry has a huge impact on biodiversity loss and climate change. With the world population constantly growing, we need to rethink the way we produce our food, ensuring high nutritional values while protecting the natural world on which we so depend.

We are all connected

During the Covid-19 pandemic, I realized how nature and mental and physical wellbeing are closely related. More and more people are redirecting

---

[*] Quality & ESG, Agricooltur

their priorities to restore and protect nature while discovering a new appreciation for health and wellbeing. Together, we are learning that everything is linked. At the same time, we can often feel disconnected from nature. We live and work in fast-growing, polluted cities that often lack quality green spaces. These urban conurbations are responsible for about 75% of GHG emissions. But they are also the beating heart of our economy and home to two-thirds of the human beings on earth. It's clear that we need to find a new way of living that can help to *preserve* nature, as well as our wellbeing.

It's an exciting challenge to rethink how our cities are designed and how they can evolve, from the creation of new urban green areas to reimagining the way food reaches city-dwellers.

Tackling habitat fragmentation and habitat loss, and the advance of invasive species, is an essential task. But the world isn't just wilderness. Urban ecosystems also play a vital role in maintaining public health (mental and physical), reducing air pollution, and providing spaces to protect against urban heat islands. They are also a source of extraordinary animal and plant biodiversity.

But the urban green spaces we need must be planned intelligently, and in a different way from what has gone before. It's about creating new spaces in which nature can be protected, and a new system in which man and nature can coexist – especially in big cities.

Indeed, cities can provide a field for experimentation, and the food system itself can play a crucial role. Imagine an urban food production methodology based on proximity: reduced use of polluting transportation, less land usage, and less usage of fertilizers. I think it is essential to give people a deeper sense of what it means to rely on nature and all the ways it helps us to survive. In this light, urban food production might be a way for citizens to feel again a real, meaningful connection with nature, as well as providing shorter supply chains and a closer bond between producer and consumer.

Our future

I am ready to tackle the challenge we are facing and contribute to helping develop a more inclusive and fairer food system for all. First and foremost, our work at Agricooltur is focused on addressing the pressing issue of water scarcity. Our future projects are focused on working even more deeply to ensure that we concentrate our efforts on reducing water waste and finding innovative methods that allow for the reuse and regeneration of this essential resource. Together with my colleagues in R&D, I am working on a project focused on rainwater recovery. Another topic we tackle as a company is the protection of soil, lessening our reliance on fertilizers and addressing issues such as groundwater pollution, biodiversity loss, and deforestation. I am committed to improving our world simply because I care. I care for the future of the life of every living being on earth. A radical change is needed, one that forces us to think in terms of not only our *own* biological life but that of the human species. This radical change will help us to see ourselves as part of a system, an *ecosystem*, in which everything and everyone plays a part.

10   Finding a path

Elisa Flamini[*]

My sustainability story began when I was just a child. I have a memory of being overjoyed when my family moved from the center of Bologna to a suburban area, filled with towering trees and sprawling common gardens. It was a place where I would spend countless happy hours. Even then, I dreamed of working in a job that would allow me to always be in contact with the great outdoors and the animals who call it home.

My parents saw my interest and encouraged me to pursue a scientific education. Eventually, this would lead to a bachelor's degree in economics and marketing. While I loved my university life, I felt that I had strayed from my one true passion: the environment.

At that time, between 2009 and 2012, it felt almost impossible to find a course that focused on sustainability or the green economy. Within the scope of my university course, the only concepts that came close were those of stakeholders and shareholders. While my business degree helped me to question extant economic and business models, I still felt something was missing.

I looked again after graduating, searching for a master's degree that would allow me to focus purely on sustainability – a word that still seemed absent from our everyday conversations. I found the search challenging, with only two courses of study that really came close to what I wanted to pursue. Eventually, this search led me to Siena and, in my second year, an exchange period at Wageningen University, an institution that is well regarded in the field of life sciences and sustainability. This experience would be decisive.

I returned to Italy after a brief internship in Germany. Even before graduating, I had been offered another internship by a huge chemical-pharmaceutical multinational. The position was within the 'Category Planning'

[*] Head of Sustainability, Green Media Lab

team, situated somewhere between marketing and sales. It was still very far from my true passion. However, finding no meaningful alternatives within the sustainability field, I set my reservations aside, feeling that the entire profession was non-existent and that people simply weren't *talking* about it. I moved to Milan with the belief that the position would at least be educational and prestigious, and that it would be silly to turn it down in pursuit of a mere 'dream.'

In fact, the experience turned out to be extremely formative from all points of view. It was an extremely complex environment, and the experience certainly gave me a set of hard and soft skills that I still carry with me today. In the meantime, I received another job offer from the multinational company Dyson.

In 2015, Dyson was not as well known in Italy as it is today. Nonetheless, the project, products, and technological innovations that they specialized in seemed incredibly exciting to me. I would end up staying there for four years, witnessing a period of incredible acceleration within the company. My professional expertise developed quickly, and I moved from the role of Trade Marketing Specialist to Retail Marketing Manager with a team of three people and the management of a EUR 6 million budget. My responsibilities grew as my acumen quickly developed, and I found myself co-responsible for the opening of new direct mono-brand stores and the full gamut of the company's consumer events. I felt that I was on my way.

Even though my career was giving me great satisfaction and recognition, I felt a nagging urgency to do what I had always been passionate about, something that would allow me to really, positively contribute, to change paradigms and develop business models that respect both people and planet.

Change

It was with this in mind that, on the cusp of turning thirty, I applied for a full-time Global MBA in Sustainable Business and Green Energy. My plan was simple: that if I secured a job, I would quit my current one and redirect my career, finally, toward sustainability. Happily, my plan worked out. Despite appeals for me to reconsider and efforts to discourage me, I left my secure career and began the MBA.

This all took place in 2019–2020, a period of not inconsiderable difficulty. But despite the challenges of the Covid-19 pandemic, I finished my MBA and began to work as a freelance sustainability consultant for Dyson, the company that I had only recently left. We had maintained a positive relationship, and my MBA aligned neatly with their own journey toward sustainability. In tandem, I began to work with a small start-up in the field of biodiversity. It was a period of uncertainty and fear, but also of great satisfaction. For the first time in my life, I felt truly fulfilled.

It was at an event dedicated to pollinating insects that I first met Green Media Lab, my current employer. From the beginning I was truly fascinated by the work they were doing as a B Corp certified communications agency, which had always been extremely attentive to environmental and social issues, having recently opened a unit dedicated to ESG (environment, sustainability, and corporate governance) strategic consulting. In January 2021, I began as Head of their ESG department, building a team of six around me. I was finally doing the job I had envisaged when I was little.

For me, working for Green Media Lab is about looking at the big picture. It means considering the entire ecosystem in which the companies, our clients, find themselves, grasping the warp and weft of interrelationships, interdependencies, and opportunities. It means finding creative and innovative solutions to face the environmental and social challenges that many companies may not yet be aware of.

In some cases, these solutions can be implemented or designed internally. When this is *not* possible, Green Media Lab supports companies in finding the right external stakeholders – from non-profit organizations to start-ups/ scale-ups, matching needs with innovative solutions. This is where professionals such as ESG consultants play an active role: supporting companies in either rethinking their processes internally or identifying the right partners, the right connections, to make change happen. That's one of the things I love the most about my job – creating meaningful connections. After all, this is the only way that we can create truly positive environmental and social impacts.

Keep running, always

At Green Media Lab, I have worked hard to build new partnerships while strengthening existing ones. For our work around Agenda 2023, I have been named an SDG Pioneer candidate in a competition promoted in collaboration with the United Nations Global Compact, an initiative that's aimed at selecting business leaders who stand out for their proactive and significant commitment to the advancement of the Sustainable Development Goals (SDGs).

In this fast-changing period in my own life, I have continued to believe that the two souls of the agency, communication and sustainability, are most powerful when brought together – that communication, when intelligently conveyed and successfully managed, has an enormous power.

Therefore, in my work, I have focused on the dissemination, internally and externally, of ethical and responsible communication as the only weapon to combat the specter of greenwashing. The data is alarming: more than half of environmental claims made in Europe have been determined to be false or misleading.

It's with this in mind that much of my work has been focused on creating tools that allow us, consumers, to become more aware of the claims and to make more responsible, informed purchasing choices. After all, individual consumer behavior has the power to change the production and supply models that companies across the world rely on. It was this work that led me to speak about greenwashing and ethical communication at UNESCO in February 2023, as well as giving presentations at several universities and business schools around the world.

In my role at Green Media Lab, I work with firms from several different industries – from fashion and agriculture to sport and technology. Because the solutions they require may be wildly different, we work closely with our creative team to provide the best possible advice. This all starts with us learning about the client, taking a snapshot of where they are from an ESG perspective. This is why assessment tools play a crucial role in the work we do. But we are always on the lookout for new and more advanced solutions.

Besides the activities we pursue with our clients, we also take care to minimize our direct impact as a communication and sustainability agency. We are committed to Net Zero 2030 and we are working on calculating, minimizing, and offsetting the carbon footprint of our business activities and events. Although we contribute lower emissions than manufacturing companies do, we *do* have an impact – often an indirect one. This is why we designed a meaningful reduction plan with ambitious goals that are being assessed in terms of feasibility.

This ongoing work ranges from investigating new ways to minimize the impact of our events to the collection of data, gathering detailed information about emissions related to every activity we are involved in.

But the journey doesn't end there. The next step will involve compensating for the emissions we make through the purchase of certified carbon credits on the voluntary market, and financing environmental and social projects that are making truly positive impacts. We have also been involved in sustainable development projects, from the building of a water well in Madagascar to the maintenance of a wind farm in India that is producing clean and affordable energy for the local population. Step by step and day by day, projects such as these will make the difference. While my journey has taken me a long way from the gardens of suburban Bologna, I am finally doing the work that I dreamed of so long ago. But that journey is far from complete.

11 The hidden costs

Estelle Beretta[*]

I was born in Reims, France, in a place famous for its champagne, and raised in a small village in the countryside nearby. My last name is Italian, as my father was born in the seaside town of Cesenatico. I had a happy childhood, spending my days and evenings playing in the forests and the fields that surrounded my little French village.

At the age of thirteen, I returned to Reims to attend boarding school, an experience of which I have many fond memories. After obtaining my Baccalaureate I went on to study at a business school in Paris before obtaining my master's degree in Caen and an MBA – across the Atlantic – in Minnesota. It was then – in 2004 – that I came back to Europe, to live and work in the Netherlands, where I have remained to this day.

Why all these details? I want to look at myself in the mirror – to look back at the twenty years behind me and the twenty that are yet to come. The person I see in the reflection is a person who was able to create positive change in the world, to advocate for the planet we *all* call home.

Growing up, neither my family nor the world immediately around me ever thought about sustainability. But its shadow could be felt. I remember how our water was polluted with chemicals by local farmers. I remember the repeated spraying of pesticides on fields and crops. But I didn't yet have the words to connect these things to 'sustainability.'

I remember once, as a young child, playing hide and seek with the children from the village. We took a shortcut through a field behind my house. When we left the fields, we noticed that our skin was stained a yellowish green and our tongues were prickling. Our mothers panicked and hosed us down. At the time I had no idea what all the fuss was about.

Other memories come to the surface. We were never allowed to drink water straight from the tap. Instead, we drank it from bottles – still and

[*] Head of Responsible Investment, APG Asset Management

sparkling – and used it for cooking pasta, making coffee, and brewing tea. Little did we know that Bisphenol A (BPA) was used in the manufacture of plastic bottles. Only now can I see the irony, how we avoided one form of chemicals while absorbing another.

When I moved to Paris for my studies, I was confronted with another ecological issue: that of air pollution. In big cities such as Paris, these clouds of smog and fuel can be overwhelming. On hot days, the whole city was thick with hot, chemical odors. I picked up the habit of wiping off the black dust that was regularly deposited along my windows. I started to develop a plethora of allergies. Later, when I left Paris, the allergies cleared up.

A bottle of water. A prickling on my tongue. The allergies I suffered. These things had a common cause that I was only beginning to become aware of.

Why?

As a child, like any kid around me, I would ask my parents: Why? The answers were often based on finance: chemicals were cheaper, lobbying was too influential, or this methodology – use of toxic materials – has always been more practical. The answers were short-term and materialistic.

As I grew up, I came to reject everything that seemed cheap, fast, and convenient. I came to understand that low prices often masked much deeper costs. I learned that the lifespan of more affordable washing machines is much shorter. In exchange for cheapness, we end up paying twice. But ultimately, it's the environment that pays.

Sticker prices are just that: sticky, and hard to dislodge. The hidden costs of 'bargains' are steep indeed, and often impossible to quantify. Individual consumers are not to blame, especially when the *real* costs are so mystified – obscured. But with proper information and education consumer habits *can* change.

We need to make the financial link between cheap goods and big environmental costs clearer. We need to educate people about supply chains and the 'real' costs of the goods we use every day: water bottles, washing machines, and so forth. So, let's go back to our humble washing machine. Let's look a little closer.

When we buy our new washing machine, the price should factor in the social and environmental impact of the raw materials used in the production of the machine. This is called 'pricing the input.' But the output should also be priced. Every product has an end of life, and recycling and reusing the parts comes at a cost. Let's use a theoretical premium of EUR 200, which would be charged for each washing machine. People who bought three machines in twenty years would be short EUR 600 versus

EUR 200 for those who bought just one, higher-quality machine in the same time period. The price of the previously 'cheaper' washing machine would now be EUR 400 higher compared with the 'expensive' one. When we factor in the output costs, the 'real' costs become much clearer.

As a part of my personal journey, I was very fortunate to meet people who educated me, led by example, and taught me how to think for myself. I found out that climate change and its negative effects are not 'news.'

As far back as the 19th century, scientists had explained how burning coal would lead to long-term negative effects. Most of the scientific findings we use today are based on findings from the 1950s. It was this research which led to the foundation of the IPCC in 1988.

Climate change pulls disaster in its wake: extreme weather conditions, the expansion of deserts, the melting of permafrost, glacial retreat, increased aridity, the increasing temperature of the oceans. It affects everything around us, from the fields of my childhood to the mountains, coral reefs, flora, and fauna of the wide world beyond.

Species relocate or become extinct due to climate change. But we may well be next. Even if efforts to minimize future warming are successful (with 'net zero' pledges), some effects will continue for centuries, ruining more and more lives.

A concrete example of these effects might be found in the writing-off of a home due to an extreme weather event – such as a flood or a wildfire. Most home insurance contracts do not cover natural disasters. They simply don't factor them in.

Another critical issue facing us is the loss of biodiversity. Biodiversity refers to the diversity of species, genes, and ecosystems on our planet, and it is essential for the proper balance and functioning of ecosystems as we know them. We are experiencing loss of biodiversity at an unprecedented rate. And the future – if we do not change our ways – is gloomy, characterized by ecological disasters, increased disease burdens, and a lack of clean air and water for animals and humans alike.

When I found out about all these facts, when I realized how big the problem was and how long it has been known, I felt upset and cheated. It's a feeling I do not want to pass on to the generations that follow us. For decades we, in the developed world, have been ignorant of the effects our lifestyles are having on the world around us.

Bobo

The more I learn, the more I feel trapped – trapped in a society that does not care for the 'long view,' nor for the people who live alongside us, nor the people who will succeed us. At times, I recognize it as a world that does not reflect my values.

So, rather than being weighed down by this knowledge, I decided to put my efforts into effecting real change.

In France, we call a person like me a '*bobo*.' It's a contraction of the words 'bourgeois' and 'bohème.' It describes wealthy, educated people who have adopted ecologically and socially conscious ways of life. And this group – these *bobos*—are on the rise, not just in France, but around the world. They are taking their consumer habits seriously, and I'm hopeful – and proud – to see the next generation taking up this mantle, slowly but surely. In how we shop and how we live, our lifestyles are changing.

In the Netherlands, where I live, people have a reputation of being careful with their money. It means they educate themselves more, before they make a purchase. They reuse and recycle. They don't throw things away – and they often buy second-hand. These behaviors may seem small, but they do have an impact.

It is important for me to put my talent, my skills, my influence, and my energy into shaping the way we live, to contribute to a "new normal" where "cheap, fast, and convenient" are not the norm but the exception. It will require considerable investment – of time and energy and resources. In the process, we will need to support developing countries in making this journey. We must make these changes *together*.

I am very fortunate and excited to work at my current organization, which is an asset manager for several Dutch pension funds. These pension funds are deeply committed to investing sustainably, which makes my work a lot easier than that of some of my peers.

Despite this big advantage, it's no walk in the park. The pipeline of young professionals looking to work in this field is still very slim. Many talented young people feel pressured to take on a 'traditional' job, and most people actively looking to make a positive contribution through their work are women.

I hope that this publication will help broaden these perspectives and generate more interest in the field. Today, I look at myself in the mirror and hope that, twenty years from now, I can look back and know that I made a difference and continue to make a difference. What of your own reflection? Think and try to find out.

12　A reason for being

Eva Zabey[*]

My passion for nature started at a young age. Although there was no single 'revelation' or lightbulb moment, I remember feeling a deep concern about animal welfare and wildlife conservation, with my Greenpeace mug and Body Shop backpack among my most prized possessions.

My dad was a sculptor and my mother worked as an independent writer for international organizations including the World Health Organization. They met in Geneva, and that is where I grew up with my two older sisters. Our family life was filled with love and creativity and shaped by a deep interest in science.

Our parents urged me and my sisters to challenge the status quo and to reject entitlement. I was encouraged to think big, to try things out, and to make meaningful contributions.

When I was thirteen, I became a vegetarian – an unusual decision at the time in Switzerland. I couldn't accept that someone would kill an animal simply for me to eat. My parents tried to talk me out of being a vegetarian, but it was a lost cause. Being determined was part of who they raised me to be.

When I was a teenager, my father introduced me to the Pugwash Conferences on Science and World Affairs, a Nobel Peace Prize-winning organization dedicated to using research and dialogue to rid the world of nuclear arms and other weapons of mass destruction. Seeing Pugwash at work gave me insight into how world leaders from both the science and policy spheres work together to find solutions behind closed doors – and how powerful that collaboration can be.

When I was fifteen, I became a Swiss Student Pugwash, mobilizing a group of passionate young people to contribute to exchanges on world af-

[*] CEO, Business for Nature

fairs. As a result, I was invited to – and participated in – two Pugwash conferences, in Norway and Mexico. I was much younger than the other youth participants, who were mostly at university and hailed from all over the world. I was impressed by their engagement and dedication as they reviewed the conference material late into the night. Together, our participation felt like real activism.

This experience gave me the confidence to start other initiatives where I could bring people together around an important challenge or common goal. I went on to set up the first-ever AIDS awareness week at my high school and, at age eighteen, I organized a student conference at CERN on topics including ethics and technology, genetic engineering, weapons of mass destruction, sustainable development, and the environment. By the time I started university I was ready to combine my passion for nature and science with my belief in the transformative power of collaboration. I studied Ecology at Imperial College in London, where I was appointed President of the Biological Science Department Student Body, in my third year. During my time at Imperial, I learned about the resilience, beauty, and fragile balance of our ecosystems, and I was particularly attracted to both lichen and limpets. It was during this time that I started to hone my public speaking, collaboration, and leadership skills.

Later, I returned to Switzerland to do a master's degree in Environmental Management at Ecole Polytechnique Fédérale de Lausanne, writing my thesis on the efforts of a large company to reduce its impact on land biodiversity.

Here, one of my professors made a comment that would shape my journey for years to come. They were dismissive of any business effort directed toward conservation. It was a belief, ardently told, that both shocked and saddened me. Coming from the mouth of a person who wielded a position of real influence, I saw this as a missed opportunity. Then, as now, I believed that business could be part of the solution, not just the problem.

It's a business case

Truthfully, the steps taken by the company profiled in my work were indeed insufficient, but they were also voluntary. I believe that businesses should be encouraged to do more to protect, conserve, and restore nature, rather than being criticized for doing too little.

From that point on, I wanted to work directly with businesses, helping them shift toward models that nurture, rather than *destroy*, nature. I began to understand that business operates within a system we are all part of, that if we wanted business to change, then we – as individuals – needed to help transform that system. This is what I have set out to do ever since.

My first professional position was an internship at the World Business Council for Sustainable Development (WBCSD). This was the start of an enlightening and fulfilling fifteen-year career. Going from intern to director, I led their work on the measurement, valuation, and reporting of natural, social, and human capital. During my time at WBCSD, I witnessed the beginning of a major transition in the corporate sustainability world. When I started, CSR efforts included some stakeholder engagement. Fundamentally, however, issues were dealt with in silos and sustainability goals were adjacent to rather than embedded *in* core business strategies. While it's by no means the norm, the situation today demonstrates how many leading companies integrate sustainability into their business and recognize the urgent need to be part of systems transformation. I was proud to have advocated and led the organization's work on corporate ecosystem valuation, which gave me the opportunity to lead the development of the Natural Capital Protocol, on behalf of the Capitals Coalition, and to speak about these issues during a TEDx talk.

Business for Nature

My time and experience at WBCSD led me to my current – and dream – job: leading the Business for Nature coalition.

Business for Nature was founded by a small group of business and conservation organizations in 2019 to bring together forward-thinking companies around a key mission: to help businesses move from being aware of the role they play in nature and biodiversity loss to advocating government adoption of ambitious policy.

The stakes driving Business for Nature's work could not be higher. Nature is in crisis. Global wildlife populations are plummeting, and irreplaceable ecosystems have transitioned from carbon sink to carbon source, endangering our ability to stabilize the climate.

The world urgently needs to reset its relationship with nature; every part of society needs to step up its efforts. And business must take a leading role. Since 2019, Business for Nature's network has grown to more than eighty partners around the world and a diverse group of businesses from all sectors, sizes, and geographies to drive credible business action and policies that will help us, collaboratively, to build a nature-positive economy for all by 2030.

It's a uniquely powerful collaboration – and it brings together everything I believe in. In our short history, thanks to an incredibly dedicated team and a truly global network of partners, companies, and financial institutions supporting our work, we have managed to unite and amplify the voice of business in nature. And momentum is building year on year.

In 2021, more than 1,400 companies in seventy countries signed our "Nature is Everyone's Business" Call to Action. In early 2022, our research and campaign on Environmentally Harmful Subsidies shed light on the scale and urgency of the changes we have to make in our socioeconomic systems. Meanwhile, our Make it Mandatory campaign, which we launched in late 2022, has been endorsed by over 400 businesses who called on policymakers gathering at the United Nations (UN) Biodiversity COP15 to make assessing and disclosing impacts and dependencies on nature mandatory for large businesses and financial institutions.

COP15, held in December 2022 in Montreal, is where all our hard work came to fruition. It remains my proudest professional moment to date. At the negotiations, Business for Nature worked with key partners to lead a delegation of around 1,000 companies – the biggest ever representation of the private sector attending a UN biodiversity conference. This unprecedented level of engagement helped shape some crucial elements of a new global deal on nature agreed at COP15, called the Global Biodiversity Framework.

In fact, I strongly believe that our Make it Mandatory campaign gave policymakers the courage and confidence to agree to one of the Framework's most transformative elements: Target 15. In effect, Target 15 sends a clear message to large businesses and financial institutions to start assessing and disclosing their risks, impacts, and dependencies on biodiversity as governments will require them to do so by 2030.

My personal highlight at COP15 was being invited to give an expert opinion in the negotiations on Target 15. My address was received with overwhelming and lengthy applause. But it wasn't my personal performance that was being applauded: it was the level of ambition and commitment from forward-thinking businesses. When I think back on my thesis and my supervisor's short-sighted comment, I can now safely say that businesses *can* have a positive impact on the natural world. The change is already happening.

Time for action, and some risk-taking

In my current role, I'm privileged to work alongside committed business leaders as they strive to accelerate their organizations' commitments to nature. Business for Nature's role is to amplify their collective voice to policymakers and the broader world. In doing so, we hope to inspire other businesses to take action and transform how they operate in a way that protects, rather than harms, our fragile and depleted planet. I do this proudly because I believe this is how we can change the system in nature's favor – and because I have three children who deserve to inherit a world where nature and people can thrive, *together*. It is this belief that drives me and – I'm sure – many of the other women featured in this book.

As George W. Bush, a former US president once said, our collective responsibility as good stewards of the environment is not just a personal responsibility. It is a public *value*. We are the first generation to fully understand the perils facing our world, and the last to be able to act.

At work and in my personal life, I always ask myself two questions when faced with a decision: is this good for the children – for their continued wellbeing on this planet? And what is the risk of *not* doing this? I believe that we – the human stewards of our planet – tend to overvalue the risk of doing something as opposed to not doing it. At this crucial time in our history as a species, we must become more comfortable in taking risks, and in investing boldly in the natural world that sustains us. We have no choice but to act. Throughout my childhood, education, and career, I have realized that inspiration and motivation come from both within and without – from our own hopes and convictions, but also from working with and learning from others. I learned this in Norway and Mexico at age fifteen. I learned it at COP15. I'm learning it to this day.

Young people today face a truly existential crisis. Each day, I'm inspired by their determination, resilience, and energy, stepping up rather than checking out. If you're one of those young people – and want to dedicate your life to building a more sustainable, equitable world – my key message is this: Find your *ikigai*, your 'reason for being.' *Ikigai* is a Japanese concept that means finding the intersection of what you love, what you're good at, and what the world *needs*. Once you have found your *ikigai*, make sure it drives everything you do. But you need to keep the big picture in mind. You need to stay flexible.

Finally, make sure you build a support network. Working in sustainability can be incredibly rewarding, but it can feel all-consuming. You should not, and cannot, take this path on your own. Learn from others and lean on them. Find sources of hope and courage wherever you can – from friends, family, colleagues, spiritual leaders, and more. After all, it is working together that will help us to become 'good stewards' of our planet.

13 Waking up

Flavie Gayet[*]

I am French, and I grew up in the countryside. My childhood memories are patterned with the sensory awakening that happens every year as the days begin to warm up, from the joyful clicking of birds that flood the spring, to the sun-heavy air and the ripe smell of the fields during the summer spreading season. The awakening of the "living world" that repeats each year, and is so pregnant in the countryside, cultivated in me a compassion for nature that I have only become aware of recently.

Early in my studies, I was guided by the desire to make a positive contribution to society. I wanted to find meaning in the work I would end up doing for the rest of my professional life. Higher education fostered my interest in world affairs and sustainable finance. In the early 2000s, this term mainly covered notions of solidarity and socially responsible finance, with green finance being in its infancy. Nature had not yet found its place in the world of finance. At best, we were talking about sustainable development at the corporate level with the search for a triple bottom line (Planet, People, Profit). So, I trained in microfinance and started a career in development finance at FMO, the Dutch Development Bank in The Hague.

Money means responsibility

Development institutions pioneered requirements to apply principles of responsible finance in developing countries because those regions were not set up with a regulatory framework sufficient to protect workers and the environment. The reputational risk in the event of bad practices was too wide. Very early on, these institutions defined methodologies for project selection and monitoring based on strict ESG criteria (environment, so-

[*] Fund Manager, Telos Impact

cial, governance). Working in this space taught me a lot about the duty of responsibility held by major financial players and their power to influence the operating practices of economic players. I learned how this responsibility could sometimes be put into action across a regulatory, legal, and social no-man's land to have a positive impact on social and environmental issues, supported by a strong commitment from local communities.

In 2010, when I was invited to the launch of the first investment fund dedicated to agroecological practices in Africa and Latin America, I understood that we were taking a new step in finance. Here, an ambitious strategy aimed to combine the requirements of private capital with the regenerative objectives of natural ecosystems. Previously, these two worlds seemed unable to coexist. On the one hand, nature belonged to the sphere of public and philanthropic funding, including nature reserves, national conservation agencies, and nature protection associations. On the other hand, private capital was at the service of traditional high-growth sectors, capable of generating sufficiently attractive returns.

Today, climate change has had deep repercussions on our natural ecosystems – with exceptionality becoming the norm in production conditions and access to resources. Along with tougher regulatory frameworks and increased consumer awareness, many sectors of the economy are now affected by the climate emergency. Natural phenomena are no longer merely a risk to mitigate in the production of raw materials. It has become a strategic matter for companies globally to preserve and regenerate natural resources if they want to secure their provision of raw materials. This goes through an unavoidable rationalization of the use of these resources in the industrial process (including the use of water and electricity) and innovative circular models. Entrepreneurs and company managers must develop more resilient business models in the face of more uncertain supply chains. Moreover, for some of companies, a positive carbon balance has become a prerequisite to capture the new outlets created by more stringent consumer demand. Environmental damage and risk have begun to impact economic issues. And a commitment to reverse or mitigate these impacts has become a key success factor for many companies. Only those who make this ecological shift will be competitive in the future in a world of scarcity of energy and natural resources.

The opportunity called nature

It is on the strength of this conviction that we decided to set up one of the first European investment vehicles fully dedicated to climate venture funds within the consulting firm where I work. We want to leverage existing quality management teams that will commit to more than one hundred environmental solutions in three years. The uniqueness of this project comes from the strike force of the capital deployed for the ecological transition, thanks to the selection of teams already active in climate strategies. Our team will also push the environmental impact requirements toward maximum alignment with the European green taxonomy. Finally, the portfolio diversification offered by the fund-of-funds structure allows us to attract private investors, many of whom have not yet taken the step toward impact investing. From this point of view, Telos has a unique position within the impact ecosystem, supporting philanthropists and investors to adopt a holistic approach to impact, to carry out their mission by using the full range of possible actions, from non-profit associations to market-return investments with impact.

I am proud to support a project that can contribute to attracting more private capital to mission-driven companies. I am also confident that more financial players will pay increasing attention to the environmental qualification in their asset allocation. In part this is because the Sustainable Finance Disclosure Regulation (SFDR) in Europe is setting strict guidelines with a common vocabulary to be adopted by asset managers as far as their environmental claims in portfolio are concerned, which should help reduce greenwashing on the financial markets. But, above all, it is because the investor community is asking for more transparency and commitment to environmental and social objectives. Therefore, in the future, asset managers will have to adopt proactive approaches in seeking best environmental practices in their portfolio in order to satisfy investors' requirements and sometimes those of a larger stakeholder community.

For example, during our fundraising process, we spoke with some university endowments that have clearly been pushed to their limits by student representatives to build a portfolio of greener investments in line with their aspirations, even though these funds generally apply a very cautious approach. Similarly, we are seeing large family foundations taking the step to impact investing by aligning their philanthropic mission with for-profit strategies in their portfolios and building consistent mission-driven portfolios with a climate focus.

In summary, my energy to act today is driven by the knowledge that the world is alive. We are living beings in our own right in the great womb of nature. We depend on the living, and it is essential for me to participate in this movement of reconciliation; humankind and the organization of our societies must operate with the living if we do not want to succumb to our own excesses. My weapon is impact investment and I put all my energy into deploying it in the fight of our generation, for the future of the planet.

14 There must be a better way

Gabriela Herculano[*]

Impatience can be a double-edged sword; it is a negative trait that can also fuel a sense of real urgency. It was with my own sense of impatience – a desire to pursue change and solve problems – that, in 2019, I founded iClima Earth, a London-based green FinTech firm. The double-edged sword had paid off.

I grew up in Brazil and obtained my MBA from the Wharton School of the University of Pennsylvania in 2002. I've spent much of my career working in the power and energy sector, structuring investments into hydro projects and renewable energy across the world.

It was a combination of age, experience, and the right time and place that enabled me to embark on this new path. Although I knew that promoting a new approach to green investments would not be easy, I also knew it would be worth it. At heart, my motivation was personal. As a mother of three children, I wanted to show my two daughters that passion and hard work would always yield positive results. I am also deeply concerned about the world I will leave behind for my son, a lovely boy with Down syndrome, who deserves a future of prosperity.

By 2019, ESG (environment, social, and corporate governance) had become a well-known acronym. But all was not well. Having worked on Wall Street for many years, I believed that capital markets could and must be a source of greatness. After all, climate change mitigation is an infrastructure problem, and the solutions require capex and R&D into what really matters. We have no time to waste on greenwashing. We can't distract ourselves with climate investments that fail to have an impact.

[*] Co-Founder & CEO, iClima Earth

Shifting the narrative: A new female-led venture

A plethora of ESG rating systems had flooded the market, with a severe divergence of scoring approaches. Investors looking to align their portfolio with climate goals could find that their holdings looked substantially different depending on whether they used MSCI, Refinitiv, or Sustainalytics data. Three clear reasons accounted for this divergence: scope, weight, and measurement. Scope pertains to the indicators chosen to represent E, S, and G, such as gender equality. Measurement is the metric used to measure these indicators, such as the number of women on the board versus the gender pay gap. Finally, weight is the relative importance given to each scope in producing the overall rating.

ESG should not equate to the use of scorecards. We will fail to maximize the impact of well-intentioned capital if we do not enhance our taxonomy and nomenclature. If the purpose of a fund is to represent companies that score very high according to an ESG scorecard, it should say exactly that. But that is how 'greenwashing' got out of hand. A fundamental shift can happen if more capital flows into the segments that support the transition to a low-carbon economy, accelerating the uptake of existing individual and system solutions while encouraging the development of new solutions to achieve them. I believe that the assessment of GHG emissions avoidance (CO_2 avoidance) will provide a meaningful quantitative measurement of the climate impact – or decarbonization potential – of 'climate champion' companies.

How women are embracing democratic investment and sustainability

Women are showing increased interest and engagement in the world of Exchange Traded Funds (ETFs)/Exchange Traded Products (ETPs). Deborah Fuhr has been in the ETF industry since 1997. She was head of investment strategy at Morgan Stanley from 1997 to 2008, then headed the ETF strategy at BlackRock in London until 2011. In 2012 she launched ETFGI – an independent research and consulting provider that maintains a comprehensive database of over 13,500 ETFs/ETPs listings, with over $5 trillion in assets.

ETFGI reported that, as of December 2020, the Assets Under Management (AUM) in ETFs and ETPs had reached a record of $7.62 trillion. But it remains to be seen if the increase in the popularity of ETFs that track market indices is due to the increase in flow from female investors. An indication of growth, on the supply side, can be found in the growth in membership of Women in ETF – WE, a not-for-profit organization founded by Deborah Fuhr in 2014 that has over 5,600 members (including myself).

There's also the fact that one of the most impressive ETF managers in the industry, in my opinion, is a woman: Catherine Wood. As CEO and CIO of Ark Investment Management, she leads a team that has created a series of actively managed ETFs that focus on disruptive innovation investing. Wood gained a lot of her popularity by predicting, back in 2018, that Tesla would be worth more than $1 trillion – a milestone which happened in November 2021.

In the field of sustainability, women are trailblazers in climate change and ESG. Barbara Buchner, founder of Climate Policy Initiative (CPI), is one of these women. CPI was founded in 2009 to support countries that are transitioning to low-carbon economies. Its team has over ninety analysts and advisors who work out of six offices around the world, all of whom have deep expertise in finance and policy.

Originally from Austria, Barbara lives in San Francisco. She holds a PhD in Economics from the University of Graz and was a visiting scholar at the Massachusetts Institute of Technology. Before founding CPI, Barbara worked at the International Energy Agency as a Senior Energy and Environmental Analyst. Prior to this she did research on climate change and policy modeling at the Fondazione Eni Enrico Mattei and was named one of the twenty most influential women in climate change and one of the one hundred most influential people in climate policy. Barbara very often speaks at high profile events worldwide, and that is how I met her – in her capacity as keynote speaker at the 2019 Green Cities event for the European Bank for Reconstruction and Development.

One of CPI's most influential contributions has been its Landscape Financing. This tracks how much of the world is investing in climate change mitigation and adaptation. Barbara has the data to allow her to make the point that the world is spending nowhere near enough on direct action to protect us against climate change, which is undermining the goals of the Paris Agreement.

She calls for more effort from every group of actors, arguing that corporations should be investing routinely in sustainable practices, that banks and investors should look for green projects and companies to build their portfolios, and that governments and other public institutions must align their efforts with roadmaps toward net zero. While Barbara sees a significant portion of total investment coming from the private sector, it is only in certain areas – where most investments provided by banks and corporations are concentrated in renewable energy and low-carbon transport, together with electric vehicle (EV) purchases by households. Public actors, especially donor governments and development finance institutions, must look to support areas where progress has been slower. Since they cannot close the investment gap alone, these actors should focus on supporting the highest impact projects that demonstrate the viability of new technologies and business models – and on creating the enabling environment to unlock other pools of capital.

It gets harder by the day

Written in 1859, Charles Dickens's *A Tale of Two Cities* starts with words that seem to speak to our own time: "It was the best of times, it was the worst of times, it was the epoch of belief, it was the epoch of incredulity, it was the season of light, it was the season of darkness, it was the spring of hope, it was the winter of despair, we had everything before us, we had nothing before us."

Our current energy dilemma at times seems unsolvable: energy security, with or without Russia, seems unattainable; affordability seems like a distant fantasy, with the price of crude oil and natural gas at record high levels; and decarbonization goals are being willfully ignored as Europe returns to burning coal at outdated power plants.

By August 2021, the energy crisis had deepened, and analysts worried about the hard choices facing us in the winter months ahead. In February 2022, Russia invaded Ukraine and threatened to stop gas flows to Europe, giving rise to fears of a new era of rationing and inflation. Economies in Europe had no choice but to turn to gas and coal production. Russia is exploiting Europe's dependence by weaponizing fossil fuels, fanning the flames of inflation in their wake. Price caps are only a palliative to the problem. To solve the supply crisis, we need to lower physical demand for fossil fuels. Are we going to drill more and disregard climate change mitigation goals? In short, are we in the worst of times? Is there any hope for the 'best?'

The future is bright, green, and sustainable

Some analysts are misinterpreting the increase in the demand for fossil fuel as a slow transition – or as no transition. The data is showing us that, from the United States and the European Union to China, we are accelerating global adoption of low emission solutions. Consumers across the world are embracing alternatives to 'business as usual,' moving away from the internal combustion engine, gas boilers, and fossil fuel-based electricity. New solutions, from EVs to telepresence, are cleaner, generate savings, and increase the predictability of supply. While fossil fuel companies are generating abnormal cash flows right now, their days are numbered.

The light at the end of the tunnel is becoming brighter, promising a future of abundant and inexpensive clean energy – of net zero buildings and cars that are more like sustainable computerized power plants on wheels. We'll create a new green hydrogen economy, solving renewable energy intermittency and building grids that are 100% green. The best of times is indeed ahead, and I am delighted to be a female voice making the point that our green future is just around the corner.

15   Packing together

*Gabriela Neves Ferri**

My name is Gabriela, and I am an engineer and mother of two. The story I want to tell today is the story of something we use constantly in our daily lives. It's the story of packaging.

While I have long held an interest in engineering, my interest in packaging started when I was just a child. Years ago, I remember watching my mother carefully wrap and package gifts for birthdays and special occasions. I became fascinated by the different materials and techniques she used, the ribbons and string and paper and tape.

After completing my studies, I began working for a major consumer goods company in Brazil, quickly rising through the ranks to become a packaging engineer. Throughout this time, I drew my motivation from the ideas and innovations that we shared as packaging experts across the food industry. But I was always *mostly* interested in the development of new 'ways' of packaging.

From my perspective, packaging has been fundamental for the evolution of society. Besides advancing the accessibility of a product, packaging speaks to us aesthetically. While the initial purpose of packages was 'simply' to portion, protect, and preserve the products they contained, they have become increasingly geared toward how they look, often with little consideration given to their environmental impact.

Change has come

I began to feel strongly that it was time to shift the focus, to find ways to make packaging more sustainable. Twelve years ago, I started discussing this idea with like-minded packaging professionals. Our common belief

* Head of Global R&D and Sustainability, All4Labels

was that the industry could make a positive impact on the environment by making small changes in the way we package our products – by changing how we work, design, and produce.

Since that time, I have been working to develop new packaging designs by incorporating innovative features focused on reducing their overall environmental impacts. These efforts have paid off. Today, I am proud to see that the discussions I had many years ago have become part of packaging regulation proposals across Europe.

Through these years, some questions have always been present. Does the reduction in the thickness of packaging material lessen its impact on the environment? How can we make sure that the packaging solutions we devise are *really* the most sustainable? This conversation used to be speculative, aspirational. I knew that something had to be done in our industry. But I also knew that the first step was to truly understand the scale of the problem.

This is where Life Cycle Assessment (LCA) studies came in. Faced with uncertainties around how to boost our collective awareness of sustainability, we decided to focus our first LCA on the environmental impact of the packaging we produce. My team, comprising many inspirational women, spent years researching and analyzing the impact of printed labels, studying everything from raw material extraction to disposal. It was a long and challenging process, but it was a crucial step in helping us to develop a comprehensive understanding of how our industry was affecting the planet.

The results of this research were eye-opening. But they also presented a unique opportunity. I realized that by developing a proprietary LCA tool, I could help the company and others in the industry to better understand the environmental impact of our products, which would help us to make more informed decisions in new packaging developments. This was our motivation to bring LCA to the next level, by expanding our database with real data from our value chain production processes.

Together with my team, I have worked tirelessly to develop this LCA tool, collaborating with researchers from universities and experts from multidisciplinary teams to ensure its accuracy and reliability. The tool was initially designed to calculate the potential impacts of pressure-sensitive labels and shrink sleeves, enabling a dynamic comparison of the environmental impact of materials and their printing configurations. The plan is to enhance the power of the tool by expanding data collection, including more materials and printing technologies. We want to build up as comprehensive a database as possible.

The LCA tool has been one of my biggest accomplishments as a packaging development leader. The next step in my professional journey was being invited,in 2021, to establish and take the lead of the global sustainability team in the company I work for. In this role, I have been responsible for driving sustainability initiatives throughout the organization and making them a key consideration in all our business decisions.

As the leader of our overall sustainability agenda, I strive to identify new areas where the company can reduce its environmental impact, such as reducing waste generation, conserving water, and transitioning to renewable energy – all while reducing emissions and sourcing sustainable materials. Wellbeing, safety, training, and development play a central role within these discussions.

It's the people

Motivating and engaging people in sustainability has been the biggest challenge in my current role. Firstly, people may have different levels of awareness and understanding of sustainability. This can affect their willingness to engage. Secondly, sustainability can be seen as too complex and overwhelming a paradigm, which may deter people from getting involved. While climate change is a global challenge that requires action on a large scale, it may be difficult for individuals to feel like their actions can make a difference. Thirdly, people may have competing priorities and interests that make it difficult to prioritize sustainability in their daily or professional lives.

To overcome these challenges, we have been creating opportunities for people to learn about sustainability in an accessible and engaging way. This includes providing clear and concise information about the issues and their impacts and showcasing examples of how we as a company and as individuals can make a difference.

Ultimately, building a sustainable future requires the participation and engagement of everyone. It is important to create a supportive and empowering environment to make this possible throughout the entire value chain. It's also important to provide opportunities for people to get involved and act, whether through individual behaviors – such as reducing waste and energy use – or collective actions such as joining community-based initiatives or supporting sustainable businesses.

With the urgent need to address climate change head-on, it is essential that companies prioritize sustainability and take action to reduce their environmental impact. It has been a gift that, in this role, I have been able to merge my personal and professional convictions, developing and implementing a comprehensive sustainability strategy that works for, and with, everyone. By prioritizing sustainability, packaging companies can not only reduce their environmental impact but also drive innovation, enhance their reputation, and create long-term value for their stakeholders.

It's our future

Looking at my two sons, I feel a personal responsibility to make a positive impact on the environment for future generations. I enjoy spending time with my family, and I often incorporate my passion for packaging into our activities, inspiring and teaching them about the importance of sorting and recycling materials, for example.

I am delighted to see that the market is changing. Today, more and more of the packaging we use addresses sustainability. I believe that we can develop packaging that is both functional and aesthetically pleasing while also being environmentally friendly. By prioritizing the use of less impactful materials and processes, we can support the transition toward a circular economy. Incorporating the LCA approach into our own sustainability strategy is just one way I can feel accountable, and I am excited to see where this journey takes us in the future.

But it's not just about packaging design. Sustainability requires a holistic approach that encompasses every aspect of our lives. The earth's resources are finite, and the effects of climate change are becoming increasingly evident. By engaging in sustainable practices such as reducing our carbon footprint, conserving water and energy, and protecting biodiversity, we can mitigate these impacts and safeguard the planet. It is our responsibility to act now, to make responsible choices in our daily lives to ensure a healthy and prosperous future for all.

My journey in packaging began eighteen years ago. More than twelve years have passed since I first became involved in product design and sustainability. I am pleased, today, to see the results coming to life. Looking back at my career, I feel grateful for the opportunities I have had to make a difference in the world. I know there is still much to be done, but I am optimistic about the future. Ultimately, I believe that by working together we can create a more sustainable world for generations to come.

16 Diving into our future

Irene Prota[*]

I am originally from Naples, a city that is defined by the sea. Water has always been an essential component of my daily routine. I learned to swim at the age of four, when my parents enrolled me in lessons at the pool for the first time. Since then, diving into the water – feeling it glide over my skin – has become an essential part of my life.

At the age of eighteen, I decided to focus primarily on my studies, almost completely abandoning sports activities. Nevertheless, the aquatic environment has always had a strong appeal, giving me a feeling of inner peace and deep serenity.

An ocean of love

A few years ago, I got in touch with 'The Life of Whales' community – a page dedicated to showcasing the beauty and rarity of certain marine mammals that are often undervalued or even mistreated.

From then on, my interest in nature escalated, particularly concerning marine flora and fauna. I became interested in understanding the workings of the seas and the oceans – a vast and fascinating terrestrial ecosystem that remains unknown to many people – a mystery. I found it admirable that there were marine biologists, scientists, and scholars who were so thoroughly analyzing a largely unexplored world that is before everyone's eyes but within reach of only a small part of the world's population. Indeed, while 600 people have visited space – and just over ten have walked on the surface of the moon – only three brave explorers have explored the Challenger Abyss, the deepest point of the Mariana Trench, some 10,929 meters deep.

We owe everything to the oceans. It was here, billions of years ago, that complex life first emerged on our planet. These were microscopic

[*] Investment professional

single-celled organisms that, thanks to evolution, would mutate into ever larger and more extraordinary creatures that today grace the ecosystems of our planet. The 'age of the mammals' is relatively recent in the long view of our planet's history, where they first appeared around 66 billion years ago. Where some walked the land – eventually giving birth to our earliest ancestors – others took to the depths of the seas.

I decided to join them, gaining my diving license in the summer of 2021. I wanted to admire, with my own eyes, the wonderful, graceful creatures that I had studied in books, photographs, and documentaries for so many years.

Below the surface, I encountered extraordinary and magnificent creatures – turtles, stingrays, dolphins, octopuses. I saw the corals that make up our seas and the ecosystems they support. During various marine excursions, I discovered how each marine creature plays a fundamental role in their ecosystem, such as the sponges and corals that provide shelter and nourishment for a wide range of marine species, or the smaller fish that clean parasites from turtles and sharks. Indeed, these smaller creatures, such as crustaceans and mollusks, also contribute to the balance of the ecosystem, helping to decompose organic matter and maintaining the quality of the water.

Another example of the underwater ecological balance is the relationship between sea turtles and algae. Turtles feed on algae, keeping their numbers under control and preventing overgrowth that can suffocate other marine organisms. This simple example shows how each species is part of a delicate balance that regulates the survival of the entire ecosystem.

The sea has taught me that every creature is important, and that every piece of debris left in the sea can have huge consequences. But I have also learned that we must act now to protect the oceans and our planet.

The sea is our life

Let me give an example that will help illustrate this vital lesson. In April 2023, a group of universities in central and southern Italy collaborated on a detailed study of the Mediterranean Sea – an area that has been particularly affected by microplastic pollution. The scientists who took part in the experiment chose the *echinoderm holothuria tubulosa* (also known as the 'sea cucumber') as their reference species, which they collected along the Salento peninsula in Apulia, southern Italy. This organism is a fundamental part of the marine ecosystem responsible for ingesting sand from the seabed, which retains microscopic organisms living in the interstices of the grains. As a result, they help to recycle organic matter.

Analysis of the intestinal contents of the reference samples not only confirmed the presence of microplastics in all the specimens analyzed but also showed that the presence of microplastics is constant throughout the year, regardless of the sampling site. This reinforces the hypothesis that microplastics are widespread and can be found in every part of our planet.

Unfortunately, this is a problem that also extends to the wider world and affects the entire food chain. Eventually, these microplastics reach human beings – contributing to serious consequences for *our* health. Today, the aquatic world is plagued by numerous crises, including water pollution, the melting of sea ice, unsustainable overfishing, and the lack of protected marine areas. These and many other issues pose a threat not only to the survival of marine species, but also to the balance of the planetary ecosystem itself.

Knowing this context, I decided to become actively involved in protecting the aquatic world by adopting a more sustainable and responsible lifestyle. One of the first things I corrected was the purchase of clothing, avoiding 'fast fashion' in favor of second-hand items. At the supermarket, I avoid buying products with excessive packaging and, wherever possible, I choose to eat plant foods rather than meat or fish.

My money and my life, where my values are

In my professional life I am an investor in the world of VC. I strongly believe that supporting start-ups engaged in green and sustainable initiatives can have a significant and positive impact on our planet. By investing in the right companies, we can support the development of innovative technologies and sustainable solutions that promote a more environmentally friendly future for us all, from the smallest of marine creatures to our very own species.

This is where my passion for sustainability and my work in VC come together. My dream is to invest in start-ups that promote the circular economy, the reduction of GHG emissions, or the protection of marine biodiversity. These represent a great opportunity to contribute to a sustainable future and common wellbeing for all. By investing in this sector, I will have the opportunity to expand my commitment to the environment, helping to grow innovative and sustainable ideas. I am convinced that more and more investors will come to recognize the importance of supporting companies committed to protecting the environment and the marine ecosystem. It is no coincidence that, in 2022, the Italian government announced a new investment fund to support start-ups and VC active in the ecological transition. The EUR 250 million budget has been earmarked precisely to stimulate the growth of the Italian innovation ecosystem, with a specific focus on the ecological transition sector.

I discovered the underwater world almost by chance – through conversations with other people, the influence of my family, and unexpected encounters with websites run by passionate enthusiasts. While I have dived only twenty meters beneath the sea's surface, this experience unleashed an intense passion that allowed me to see the marine world with new and different eyes. Gaining a first-hand understanding of its grace and its complexity, I also came to understand just how dire the situation is, from the microplastics that have entered the food chain to the tragic bleaching of corals.

I am determined to preserve these ecosystems while we still have time and to defend our planet – not just the oceans, but also the forests and fields. I am ready to take a leading role in the fight for our future, knowing that marine life not only enchants us with its beauty, but is also essential for our very survival. My passion for the sea has become a mission of love and a life mission: to safeguard the wonderful world that I call home.

17 For a sustainable and collaborative finance

*Isabelle Combarel**

I grew up in the Nouvelle-Aquitaine region, in the southwest of France – a region suffused with the smell of Landes pines and sea spray. We spent our weekends as a family exploring the natural world around our home, listening as much to the silence of the mountains as to the songs of the migratory birds that flew over the Arcachon Basin – and to the storks.

At a very young age, I was made aware of the wonders of nature but without being aware of how delicate the balance was between fauna, flora, and humans. At the time, few people realized what was happening before our eyes: our world was being threatened by human-caused climate change. The IPCC did not exist, and the Kyoto Protocol was many years from being signed. When I chose my career path, I was not aware of this new paradigm, of a 'finite' world with global limits.

As a student at the University of Economic Sciences in Bordeaux, I became passionate about economics, including financial markets and the stock market. I knew, without a doubt, that I wanted to work in finance.

MAIF

After obtaining my degree in finance and international trade, I joined the French mutual insurance company MAIF as a financial research officer. This experience was decisive for me, for it was here that I developed the convictions that would shape my career even to this day.

Created in 1934 in a context of economic crisis, MAIF wanted to provide independent and supportive insurance for teachers. It was a new and different model, one based on efficiency and trust. At the origin of this social economy model, MAIF accompanied the birth of three other mutuals,

* Deputy CEO, Swen Capital Partners

dedicated to the insurance of craftsmen (MAAF), merchants (MACIF), and local authorities (SMACL).

It is no coincidence that, in 2020, it became a company with a mission, setting out to serve the common good. I still remember my job interview. I had applied for a position related to stock markets. Hanging behind my two interviewers was the latest MAIF advertising campaign, reading "our values are not listed on the stock exchange." It was a few years later that I understood the full power of this message. MAIF's commitment is real, and it has been proved time and time again in my daily work life.

I joined MAIF at a very particular historical moment – in October 2001, a month after the World Trade Center attacks, eighteen months after the bursting of the internet bubble, and a matter of days before the Enron fraud scandal broke. Facing the full extent of the failure of the markets, MAIF wondered if the money entrusted to it by its members could be invested in a more ethical and responsible way, not only to generate financial performance, but also to have a *meaning*.

In 2004, we embarked on a new and unfamiliar path – that of SRI (socially responsible investment). This marked a real turning point for me, transforming my vision of what finance could *do* in the world. Beyond the numbers and the markets, I could see new opportunities to get involved and to do good. Through our voting rights as shareholders, we could and can move the needle.

In the ten years I spent at MAIF, I immersed myself in these values – new and old – and built my own vision of my job as a financier. It became clear to me that I – that we – could stay true to our convictions, that we could contribute to the emergence of a *different* form of finance, one that was truly sustainable.

Me time

It was through MAIF that I met Jérôme Delmas, with whom I helped build what would become SWEN Capital Partners in 2015. Driven by my convictions and compelled by the idea of inventing new finance practices, in 2012 I joined a "small business unit" attached to OFI Asset Management.

This move marked both a professional and a personal challenge, with my office in Paris and my husband and two young children in Niort. As early as 2012, and well before the generalization of this practice following the Covid-19 pandemic, I was already experimenting with 'teleworking' two to three days a week. It was an exciting and energizing challenge that allowed me to get away from the very short-term volatility of the stock markets. During this time, I discovered the long-term nature of the unlisted market, which supports the 'real economy' of companies and concrete projects. I thus saw it as an ideal framework to encourage the integration of extra-financial, environmental, and social issues with the managers we were working with.

However, the SRI and ESG dimensions had not yet penetrated the hushed and very masculine spheres of the unlisted sector. When I proudly announced my intentions in front of the players on the market, I received, most of the time, only an amused look that seemed to convey the feeling that "it will pass." I thought – I *knew* – differently.

Together with Jérôme Delmas, Jean-Philippe Richaud, and Hervé Aubert, I was convinced that our project was the right one: to become one of the leaders in responsible investment in the unlisted sector and to support companies in making these changes. To support this ambition, I recruited ESG experts and, in 2018, created a dedicated team that was independent from the investment teams, reporting directly to general management. This strategic decision to internalize this expertise and have the freedom of analysis and levers for action has always been a strong differentiating factor in the unlisted sector. All our choices and actions have been, and still are, led by one guiding principle: to invest responsibly based on objective criteria while always demanding ESG analysis. My role within SWEN has quickly become more than just a 'job': it is a project in which I am fully invested, the vehicle that allows me to fully materialize my convictions and commitments.

Together, within SWEN, we have built a new and different model in our sector, one that doesn't fit into any box and that continually challenges the status quo. At the time, the words 'management company' and 'commitment' still seemed antinomic, but we proved that, on the contrary, commitment could indeed fuel performance. And to those who told us that ESG was only a risk management approach, we demonstrated that it is in fact a value creation strategy. This is one of the reasons why we created the 'ESG Best Practices Honours, by SWEN' just ten years ago: to share, promote, and value virtuous ESG and CSR practices, and to encourage as many people as possible to take action.

What drives me is not my personal interest but rather the collective, collaborative encounters I share with passionate people with sincere values. My goal is to bring as many people on board as possible, building, together, a shared path for the common good.

Our time: Creating a movement

This is why, in 2012, I joined what was then the AFIC sustainable development club, which has now become France Invest – our professional association. I participated in the creation of its sustainability commission and remain an active member of its steering committee. It is in this same spirit that I have chosen, outside of SWEN, to work with players with whom I align my values, such as Sofiouest – the financial investment company of the French media group OUEST France – which works to defend the freedom and independence of the press and of which I am a member of the Board of Directors.

For more than ten years, between Paris and Bordeaux – where I returned with my family in 2018 – I have contributed to the growth of SWEN as much as it has allowed me to live my commitment, to question it, and to reinforce it continuously. This was particularly the case during the COP15 in Montreal, in December 2022. At SWEN we had been dealing with climate issues since 2017 and with biodiversity issues for only a few months, considering them as two parallel issues without knowing how to concretely link them. It was during COP15 that I really became aware of the importance of integrating biodiversity into the heart of our strategy without further delay, but also of the need to address it *alongside* climate. It no longer makes sense to think of 'climate' on the one hand and 'biodiversity' on the other; we must now think of 'nature.' This is why we have decided, within SWEN, to develop a new policy for Nature, to be published in June 2023.

I was proud of what we had already achieved, but I knew it was not enough. To maximize our impact, we had to go further, to transform our model to make it more contributory and empower it to carry our *entire* commitment. This is why, in March 2023, I launched a significant change in our business operations and our investment approach in order to contribute to the emergence of *truly* sustainable finance.

Framed by regulations, practices in the field of sustainable finance are far from being aligned. While everyone can claim to be a sustainable finance player, we wish to give new strength to this expression. Moreover, while money is a lever for change, money alone cannot do everything. This is why we have decided to commit ourselves not only through the investments we make, but also by setting up a new dedicated operational and strategic governance structure and by mobilizing our teams and our ecosystem to guide our clients, our investments, and our partner management companies along a common and virtuous path.

For me, the collective is the key to success. To make a meaningful change and a real contribution, finance needs its driving forces to cooperate. It is not a question of eliminating all the competition, but rather of knowing how to pool our assets in the face of the global challenges we all face. This is the meaning of my work on the Board of Directors of France Invest – the French association that brings together all the private equity players.

In my work, I have always promoted a collaborative and committed vision of working together for the benefit of the planet and the people who call it home. I know that we will go further, together. After all, SWEN cannot meet the challenges facing our planet alone. If the forests of my childhood are to be preserved; if the vineyards of Bordeaux are to continue to produce the wines that intoxicate us; if nature is to regenerate; and, as António Guterres, Secretary-General of the United Nations, reminded us, if we are to build a common future for all living things, we must act together.

18   Change comes slowly

*Julia Hoglund**

I have battled with imposter syndrome throughout my career, from university graduation to my current role, seven years later, as a Sustainability & Strategy Director. And I feel it as I write this, knowing that my chapter will be bookended by the stories of remarkable women who have achieved and contributed so much, and who inspire me daily. And I ask, how can I contribute?

In a way, this mindset reflects how a lot of us feel about climate change – overwhelmed by the daunting collapse of ecosystems and growing inequalities. How can we make a difference that feels impactful in the face of the global problems we collectively face?

All I can write about is what I know. I have a background in finance and corporate sustainability – and I have always been curious to understand behaviors and how to trigger change or transformation. As a sustainability advisor to some of the largest companies in the world, my time is filled with carbon reduction planning, making the business case for the shift to more sustainable practices, and being on speed dial to executives who have investors to answer to. It's a meaningful job, but not something my eight-year-old self might have imagined I would dedicate my life to. Back then I cared about saving dolphins but didn't understand how that would happen. My role is to help make incremental changes happen through business decisions, which over time can help navigate a better course for the proverbial ship we all sail on. It is never easy, and transformative change rarely happens as quickly as we want or need it. But I would like to share some of my observations, thought processes, and the strategies that have guided me. And if I can inspire someone to start a career in sustainability and to feel like they are making their own positive footprint on the future, then this will be a success.

* Sustainability Strategy Advisor

Small steps matter

This sounds like a well-trodden path, but bear with me. I want to start here because the idea of 'incremental change' gets a lot of flak. People in sustainability tend to criticize this idea for not moving fast enough, or not being bold enough. Of course, I still subscribe to the pathways of net zero emissions and ending all types of discrimination. And I understand that incrementalism can be viewed as a smokescreen for the corporate world. But in my experience, what businesses of today need most support with is not the what, or the why. It's the how.

That is why, when speaking about the big challenges we face and the changes we need to make, I try to focus on the first few steps businesses can take in the right direction. Who should we speak to? What do we need to measure? And what do we need to achieve this year to move the needle? This makes it easier and far less daunting to execute. In a day-to-day context, being effective is about making small decisions and small changes at a business level. This simple idea is a strong motivator for me when I am at work grinding through a report, assessing carbon data, or preparing a workshop. This is it; this is what change looks like. I know it's not sexy, but it's true. It's easy to forget, but when I find myself feeling powerless, I think about the fact that grand decisions, innovations, and movements all started with one fact, one conversation, or one idea. It feels like we are waiting for a silver bullet, but we need hundreds, even millions of small steps to set us in the right direction. And in a strange way, this gives me the energy to power on.

Business equals people

If change can spring from one fact, conversation, or idea, that means that it can start with one individual. Understanding that businesses are about people, and learning to speak their language and communicate well, is the core of helping empower change.

It's all well and good to know the science (and I would highly recommend everyone read and understand the latest IPCC report and the concept of the planetary boundaries). But the point of contact to inspire change is usually through person-to-person interactions. It's about learning to persuade and communicate effectively, whether that be pitching presentations, writing articles, or having a conversation with colleagues over coffee. Communication is often overlooked, but honing these skills makes a big difference because corporate sustainability is often about convincing others to make difficult decisions. It's about making things a little easier and a little smarter – not being overwhelming or too forceful.

As a graduate, I thought of myself as an activist in a suit, stepping into boardrooms and telling them to wake up (both figuratively and literally). This didn't go down so well. My greatest lesson is that you need to be a critical friend and problem solver and deliver suggestions and solutions in a bite-sized, simplified, and visually inspiring way. You need to present clear actions and responsibilities to make it easy for decision-makers to just nod their heads and say yes. So never underestimate a punchy tagline and a smart-looking strategy visualization – and don't be afraid of simplifying the complexity of it all. They don't need to know everything all at once.

What is value?

Now we're getting into the nerdy stuff. This is my real passion. In the current context of corporate sustainability and ESG agendas, there are many different approaches. One is to tick boxes and catch up with the latest regulations and ratings, and this is important, but it's also backward-looking. It often focuses on mitigating risk to protect short-term profits.

Another approach is looking forward, looking at how we define value. How do we create the maximum value for *all* stakeholders – customers, supply chain workers, employees, communities, and shareholders? How can we predict the landscape in the future to make the best holistic decisions today? This can sometimes come across like an ideology or political belief, but it's all about long-term success and resilience.

A few recent studies have articulated the connection between sustainability practices and business success:

- Products making ESG-related claims averaged 28% cumulative growth in the period 2018-2022, versus 20% for products that made no such claims.
- 63% of Gen Y and Z consumers are more attracted to brands that source services and materials in highly ethical ways.
- Companies at the forefront of sustainable procurement generate 3% higher margins than those that don't focus on their suppliers' ethics, environmental, and labor practices.
- 60% of employees choose a place to work based on their beliefs and values.
- Executing ESG effectively can help combat rising operating expenses (such as raw material costs and the true cost of water or carbon), which can affect operating profits by as much as 60%.

But even with a clear business case, the biggest challenge is the constant battle between short-term profit and sustainable value creation. Considering this, something that is becoming more and more common, and something I work a lot with, is to integrate social and environmental values into the way companies measure and communicate performance and progress. For example, many companies have started to put an internal price on carbon emissions – which they use to evaluate the success and return on investment of future projects. Others are integrating diversity goals into executive remuneration. And there are many emerging regulations, reporting frameworks, and standards that aim to create balanced accounts, where environmental and social values are monetized or measured next to financial performance. This is the future, and it's exciting.

Brave leadership

Will a holistic way of measuring value, good-looking slides, and small incremental steps in the right direction be enough to save us? One missing, binding ingredient is brave leadership. It takes courage to challenge the short-termism of corporate behavior and to stand up for and make decisions based on what's morally, ethically, and emotionally right.

This is where I am hopeful. Thinking about what the next generation of business leaders will look like, in terms of diversity of thought and sustainability awareness (and climate anxiety!), keeps me optimistic. The opportunity here for women and other minorities is vast. According to a large 2021 study across forty-six countries, 20% of the 3000 companies involved had a dedicated sustainability officer in their senior leadership team, and 45% of those positions were held by women. In the United States, there has been a 94% increase in female senior sustainability leadership in the period 2012 – 2022.[1] So, as we are climbing the corporate ladder, women are stepping into the rooms where the real decisions are made, progress is evaluated, capital is allocated, and value is defined.

So, am I making a difference? I really think I am. I may not be a climate unicorn founder and I haven't personally saved any dolphins (yet), but maybe that's exactly the point – to make ESG as normative and mundane as accounting, finance, and risk management; to make it a natural part of conversations about growth, innovation, and talent acquisition. By not making sustainability the siloed black sheep of corporate behavior, we have a real

---

[1] Weinrib Group (2021), *The Chief Sustainability Officer 10 years later. The rise of ESG in the C-suite*

chance to make it simply the way we do business. And that, I am convinced, is our biggest chance to make a real, incremental, and long-term impact. I am optimistic that the future, diverse, climate-anxious leaders are the ones that will get us there.

Maybe I'll be one of them – if my imposter syndrome allows.

19   Swimming against the tide

*Karen Boers**

We have been dependent on our 'tribes' and communities for our survival for as long as we have been on this planet. And it's not just humans that benefit from a connected sense of belonging; recent research shows that this is the case for all mammals. The safer we feel, the easier it is to unlock our higher cognitive functions. Once we sense danger, either real or perceived, these higher functions shut down. We mastered the ability to quieten our fight or flight responses ... until we didn't.

I believe that the only way forward is to remember that we are dependent on each other for our survival – not just as a species but on an individual level. Cultivating a sense of belonging and safety is fundamentally necessary for our psychological and physical wellbeing. My mother's work was guided by this conviction. She taught with a feverish passion and provided a safety net for teens who were left with no options and nowhere to turn. She died when I was thirteen years old, and since then I have dedicated my life to living up to her example.

Help

Naturally, I followed in her path and studied to be a teacher, in Belgium, only to find out that the school system was too rigid for my taste. So, I turned to the private sector, starting out in the human resources industry, trying to help blue collar job seekers find a suitable position. After a few years, I joined a new Flemish software innovation center that focused on applying academic research to benefit society. Experts across disciplines and universities joined forces to work with the people who would directly benefit from the solutions they were trying to build. It opened my eyes to

* Social Entrepreneur & Managing Director, FARI

the potential of using technology as an accelerator to improve people's lives while safeguarding ethical, legal, and regulatory boundaries. As marketing director, I was situated smack in the middle of a huge network of academic, public, and private sector actors, all connected by a mission to solve complex societal challenges in healthcare, mobility, media, and so forth.

It was an exciting time of discovery, building bridges and helping to bring those innovations to market through research partners and spin-off companies. One of the projects that has stuck with me was a solution designed for sick children in long-term treatment, to help them continue with their schooling and stay in touch with their friends – by chatting and playing games in a digital playground. In the pre-social media era this was an incredible project to be a part of. And the glow in the eyes and the smiles of the three patients that participated in the trial was enough to keep us going for years.

We then extended our support to other start-ups looking to disrupt and innovate, through an incubation and acceleration program and a pre-seed investment fund. I came across dozens of entrepreneurs who were passionate about solving societal problems and helping others overcome similar obstacles. I came to realize that most of these innovators weren't in it for the money, but because they were frustrated by a particular problem and they saw a solution that many people could benefit from. Dozens of entrepreneurs in our community were looking for the next market(s) to enter, the right go-to-market partner, and smart money to make it happen, while trying to overcome the many practical and administrative obstacles they came across. Many of them looked my way to help them connect and build meaningful relationships.

The jump

At the same time, my private life took a twist, and I started a relationship with an entrepreneur and blended our family and five young children together. He encouraged me to follow my calling and to jump into the adventure of becoming an entrepreneur myself – it seemed to be the best way for me to continue serving my mother's memory. With the help of a dozen tech entrepreneurs and investors, I created the national start-up community Startups.be, the first of its kind in Europe. The network helped connect hundreds of start-up teams to incubators, accelerators, and investors across the country and supported the international market through discovery missions in start-up hot zones, first in Europe and then beyond.

Following their call for more entrepreneurial friendliness across our layers of government and following the lead of Neelie Kroes, European Commissioner for Digital Agenda at the time, we amplified their voices through the Belgian Start-up Manifesto (http://startupmanifesto.be/) and exerted whatever influence we had through the media and with politicians to drive positive change. The tax shelter for angel investment emerged, taxes on first hires were lowered, the ban on night labor was finally lifted in the e-commerce industry, and maternity leave for women working independently was extended. With many other European countries following suit, we saw an opportunity to also amplify critical messages and influence policymakers at the European level, which was especially important for fast-growing scale-ups expanding across member states at high speed and in dire need of a European digital single market – which, I must add, still does not exist, although we tried, and succeeded, in some other areas. The European Scale-Up Manifesto caught the attention of multiple EU Commissioners, and start-ups became more than a fringe topic. An understanding grew that these companies had the potential to boost and disrupt entire industries and therefore should be recognized.

With pan-European collaboration between start-up communities becoming the norm, we solidified those partnerships through the creation of the European Start-up Network. The network comprises thirty-eight national start-up associations and represents more than 30,000 validated start-ups. It's entirely bottom-up and so it's a force to be reckoned with. National partners started supporting the go-to-market of their befriended communities, which is a thousand times more effective than trying to enter your companies in another market. Investors were drawn to the high volume of promising companies, and matchmaking events emerged across Europe.

We saw a surge of positive change, and many entrepreneurs in the network still reach out to each other, and me, when in need of peer feedback or support. There was only one field where we saw no progress, and that was the war for talent. High-potential start-ups were being outbid by the big companies, who in turn were snatching talent away from each other, creating an everlasting and disastrous bidding cycle and an unprecedented employee turnover rate, resulting in high cost and low return on investment – if you could find staff at all.

During my last international start-up mission, we visited a coding school in Kenya that opened my eyes to the fact that technology has become widely accessible and potentially transformative. I realized that with a good dose of enthusiasm and grit, a laptop, and an internet connection, anyone can learn how to code. This can be a very powerful way of helping people out of poverty or other dire circumstances because stable employment is the most sustainable way out and typically benefits not just the individual but also their entire family.

Creating the future from the bottom up

I knew I needed to fight for this cause – helping people who weren't born with the opportunities in life that many of us in Western Countries were. This was a bridge worth building and came with the co-benefit of growing the talent pool for our companies that were under threat of losing the global race due to being substantially understaffed. It meant swimming against the tide, as education, employment, and innovation are regionalized matters in Belgium, and to make this work, I absolutely had to draw on the economies of scale. We decided to seize the opportunity and create BeCode in collaboration with the French coding school Simplon, so we could hit the ground running.

We started out by running junior web developer training in Brussels, and within five years we had trained over 2,500 job seekers in web development, artificial intelligence, and data science, as well as the fundamentals of cybersecurity, in five cities across Belgium. Thanks to a strict selection process to identify the most motivated applicants, drop-out rates were very low and almost seven out of every ten graduates found long-term employment within six months of graduating. Learning as we went and with many hiccups along the way, a fifty-person-strong team battled every single day to build strong partnerships with the public employment agencies and with industry partners looking to hire. The Covid-19 pandemic shook us, but the European network of coding schools that emerged shifted gear overnight and enabled remote learning with similar efficiency.

Some of the stories of our graduates will stick with me for the rest of my life. There was the refugee woman who survived eighteen months in the most dangerous circumstances getting to our country, learning the language and a new profession before she was reunited with her children. Or the nurse who worked for twenty years and saw her career end because of back problems. She thought her life was over, until she understood that her curiosity for new technologies could help her find a new path. Or the truck driver who suffered a terrible childhood and was kicked out of school for rebellious behavior, who then lived with regret for many years before convincing us he deserved a second chance.

Pause, then go

Leaving the project was one of the hardest decisions I ever took, but it was time for me to recharge my batteries and move on. Entrepreneurial life can be nerve-racking, with little room to catch your breath and almost no safety net in place to break your fall. For employees, the high pace and weighty expectations create a constant sense of risk that becomes almost impossible to bear over time. During my time off I realized this is where I could serve next – to help create a safe place for people to catch a breath, reground, connect to nature, and reboot as an even better version of themselves. So, my partner and I bought a small farm and set out to start a care farm for anyone battling chronic stress and burnout. It's just in the starting phase, but after visiting a few wonderful projects with similar purposes and realizing its full potential, we're quite excited about it!

In the meantime, I did not abandon the potential of technology. When I was invited by former colleagues from the research center to join FARI, the AI Center for the Common Good that was created by the two Brussels universities, I realized this was where all my previous experience converged. It allows me to build bridges between academic research and expertise and society to help both the public sector and companies to innovate through these state-of-the-art technologies, including the creation of life-long learning programs and supporting entrepreneurship in this industry. Helping the public administrations to truly transform and support policymaking in the field could turn out to be a fantastic lever for improving the lives of citizens, communities, and companies. The unique Brussels environment, with layers of government from local to European, packed into a few square kilometers, with thousands of companies and a multicultural and multilingual community of citizens wrapped around it, seems like the perfect living lab to strike the balance between technological advancement and cautious safety. I am sure it will not be the final stop in my journey, but it feels like a good place to serve for quite some time to come!

20   The path toward impact

Laura Blanco[*]

It took me several attempts until I found my way into the world of impact investing.

The phrase 'impact' means different things to different people, presenting one of the main challenges for investors. In truth, impact can only be defined by the people or environments most affected by it. But these actors rarely have a voice. From my perspective, impact is about using the power of finance and investment to transform people's lives, to achieve real change on a net positive basis. Impact means achieving balance through purpose. And I have been searching *for* that balance ever since I started working in finance and investments.

I graduated from the Stern Business School at New York University in 1996, starting a job on the sell side as an equity research analyst in New York. I worked endless days, managing to move steadily up the ladder. My career was on a very solid footing, but I had little time to think about anything other than work. In time, I was promoted to senior analyst, a job that saw me travelling around Latin America and the United States to visit companies' operations while meeting with senior management and large investors.

Coming from a mid-size town in Spain, life in New York City was hectic, tough, and exciting, full of interesting opportunities and people. I felt I was at the center of the world, and that I had it all: health, money, friends, love, a great job. That was until I hit my eighth year as an analyst and realized – with a start – that something was missing. Sadness and dissatisfaction followed me like a shadow. I couldn't make sense of it. Those were restless days indeed.

---

[*] Global Head of ESG, Santander Wealth Management and Insurance

Awakening

Losing my sister to cancer, at the age of forty-three, in 2004, was a wake-up call. I started exploring a change in job and even a change of country, thinking that going back home – and into a different position – would provide the solution I was looking for. It was not until many years later, when I heard Mohamed Yunnus talking about the importance of having a purpose and read *The Purpose of Capital* by Jed Emerson, that everything clicked.

Several years before, in 2000, I had started reading about microfinance, but it seemed to me almost impossible to make the switch from a job in Wall Street. I felt that I wasn't brave enough to make the leap. Later, in 2004, I came across Pro Mujer.

Back then, Pro Mujer was a small charity that had launched in 1990 to run microfinance operations mostly in Bolivia and Peru, with an ambition to expand to the province of Salta in Argentina. As of 2023, Pro Mujer has empowered more than two million women across the region and has granted $4.4 billion in microcredits.

I made my opening by cold-calling the head of marketing of Credit Suisse Asset Management in New York, who was a Pro Mujer board member. I chose her because I had read that she had made her own career change from research into marketing. My approach worked, and she introduced me to Carmen Velasco, the woman who co-founded Pro Mujer in 1990 with the mission to empower women through a combination of community building, micro loans, access to health, and education. I was on the cusp of joining but instead decided to quit my job and return to Spain to pursue a career in a start-up I had invested in earlier – a move that would eventually take me to Hong Kong.

Re-route

There were some positive benefits of this move, but in hindsight it was a mistake that pushed me further and further away from finding my purpose.

It was only later, in 2018 – after building a $1 billion pipeline of deals in private markets in Latin America while working at Nakatomi Capital – that I decided to google for a volunteer job in sustainability. That search opened a door onto the unknown and led me into the world of impact investing.

What struck me most about this world was the openness of the people who worked in it, all of whom were working toward a common goal. This was not something I was used to in the world of finance and investing.

During my initial foray into impact investing, I came across several initiatives that were taking place at the time and have been key to the development of the field: the Impact Management Project (IMP), social impact bonds, and the Global Steering Group for Impact Investment (GSG). The IMP, which later evolved into the Impact Management Platform, was a collaboration between more than 2000 organizations in the impact investment ecosystem (accelerators, investors, intermediaries, foundations, consultants) working to agree on how to measure impact for investments. I was able to call in to their 'huddles' and listen to live discussions on how to approach the measurement of impact. It was an exciting time.

I was also hooked by social impact bonds and couldn't stop reading about this fascinating tool – a means of structuring an investment through public and private collaboration to tackle pressing social challenges such as homelessness and NEETS (young people that are not in employment, education, or training).

Historically, financial innovation has been triggered by regulatory constraints that were limiting the amount of profit that could be generated. A clear example of that was the 2008 financial crisis. The need to solve social challenges as a trigger for financial innovation rather than pure greed was a revolutionary concept to me.

Finally, I managed to join a group of amazing people who had pioneered impact investment in Spain and who were building the Spanish National Advisory Board for Impact Investment (SpainNAB). Their goal was to join the GSG, a major ecosystem of market builders who are championing impact investment in their countries, generating and spreading knowledge, and sharing best practices.

At around the same time, I joined Social Starters, a three-month volunteer mentoring program out of the United Kingdom that matched social start-ups with experts who could support and assist them. I was matched with Gus Zogolovitch, founder of Unboxed Homes, who had just launched Crowdestates – a crowdfunding platform specializing in secured lending for property projects with a community or social benefit.

Since activity in property development is in the hands of a few large developers, and gentrification caters predominantly to foreign investors, rents and living costs in London have shot up dramatically, kicking lifetime dwellers out of their communities and creating ghost neighborhoods in the process. The idea behind the project was to offer investors the opportunity to help smaller innovative developers to make buildings for sustainable and cohesive communities.

Gus was the most optimistic person I had ever met, and his positive energy was endless. We worked together to set up a theory of change and an impact measurement framework for Crowdestates using the IMP's "five dimensions" as the guiding norms, helping us to select projects that could qualify for finance. It was an amazing challenge to put the theory into practice, involving many hours of research to scientifically document the causality between home building and development as drivers for wellbeing and community cohesion.

Money as a weapon for impact

After this period of mentoring, I realized that going back to mainstream finance was out of the question. This was why, in the summer of 2018, I joined Foro Impacto, the secretariat that a year later would become Spain-NAB. This gave me the chance to meet incredible pioneers of impact investing in Spain from whom I learned a lot. I am very thankful to Maria Ángeles León from Open Value Foundation, Agustín Vitórica from GAWA Capital, Luis Berruete from Creas, Ángel Pérez Agenjo, and José Luis Ruiz de Munain, the director of SpainNAB, among many others.

We were a small group who wanted to make a difference. After many working sessions and conversations with the domestic impact investment ecosystem, we agreed on an agenda with five workstreams that involved the entire value chain of investments – and the public sector – to develop the market for impact investment in Spain. Some of those workstreams focused on innovative structuring for impact, such as blended finance vehicles, fostering social impact bonds, and developing a culture of measurement for impact management, all with the overarching goal of channeling more money from the private, public, and third sectors in a collaborative manner to scale the market. As of December 2021, the Spanish impact investment market amounted to EUR 2.4 billion, of which EUR 436 million is from private markets. These have grown more than fourfold since we started sizing the market in 2018.

As director of knowledge and outreach for SpainNAB, I had the privilege of meeting inspiring people who were dedicated to generating impact. Their work has shown that things *can* be done differently. Our main challenge, in all of this, was to build credibility among mainstream finance incumbents and the third sector, which still has a silo mentality that limits the scaling of impact.

The Covid-19 pandemic hit us just nine months into the job. We were agile and moved all the activity and events planned for the year to a virtual format so we could continue with our mission. Covid-19 ended up being a tailwind for us, not only because it raised awareness of sustainability and impact but also because we were able to attract a wealth of speakers who would have been unlikely to fly to Spain for a physical event but were happy to participate in our task forces remotely.

There are many things I'm proud of from my time at SpainNAB. Among these are the three toolkits we produced to generate knowledge and bring international best practices in impact investing to the domestic context. The toolkits are now being used by people across the country and in vastly different sectors, including by some international experts with a long trajectory in the field such as BidInvest. One of the main takeaways from those days is that impact investment can have many angles or definitions, but it boils down to three things: innovation, collaboration, and determination to change our mindset.

Just over a year ago, I joined Santander as their Global Head of ESG in their Wealth Management & Insurance division. With more than EUR 400 billion of managed funds between the private banking and asset management businesses, Santander ranks among the top players in the industry. The power of such a platform to transform the way we invest is huge, and this is precisely why I made the move. Having moved from impact to ESG investing, I believe I can bring much to the table. But there is no set 'pathway' for impact investment to follow. The journey is our own to make.

21 In pursuit of purpose: A life shaped by love, luck, and the odd plane crash

*Leslie Johnston**

I grew up in a place named after the natural phenomenon of the Aurora Borealis. Despite the illuminating name, Aurora, Illinois, lacked the excitement of nearby Chicago. But it did offer something at which nondescript towns in the middle of the United States tend to excel.

Stability

This lack of excitement was reinforced by my mother, a homemaker who always had my back. She was always one to do what is right and not necessarily what is easy. She fought for me when I needed her. As a result, I felt trusted, loved, and supported, even when I made decisions she may not have agreed with.

But my world was small, if not insular. And I had an itch to escape it. As a young girl, I collected postcards, usually scooped up from local garage sales. I remember spreading these images of faraway places on my bedroom floor, trying to figure out where Andorra was. Or Ghana. Or Bahrain. I imagined what life was like in these distant lands. When it came time to apply to universities, I chose options that were far from my hometown, landing on one that was 3425 kilometers away, near the California coast.

Over the next ten years, I had numerous experiences that helped shape who I am today, all of which I am grateful for. I was lucky enough to study at L'Institut d'Etudes Politiques in Grenoble, France. I managed to land a summer job working as the baker in the staff cafeteria of an Alaskan fishery. I hitchhiked my way through the Middle East. I became obsessed with the Russian language and temporarily lived with an elderly couple on the outskirts of Moscow. I ultimately completed a Master of Science degree in

* CEO, Laudes Foundation & Chair, EVPA

Foreign Service but turned down an offer to start a career as a diplomat. I also met the love of my life at the young age of twenty, parted ways for a decade, and married him at thirty-one (we're still married, twenty years later).

When I reflect on my journey to date, four moments stand out as important turning points for me.

1998: The awakening

After graduate school, I accepted a role with a management consulting company, where I mostly worked with financial services clients. My days were filled with the titillating tasks of creating pivot tables and pulling out insights from data. And then, quite unexpectedly, I was sent to South Africa, where the company was building its first office.

It was an extraordinary time, just a few years after apartheid was dismantled, and the country was being reborn on a foundation of hope and forgiveness. I couldn't even begin to understand the deep injustice of apartheid – and the fissures it created across South African society – but I certainly felt it, even during this time of deliberate dialogue via the Truth and Reconciliation Commission. I also felt the deep chasm between the haves and the have nots; just outside my office, it was not unusual to see, next to a brightly lit TGI Friday's restaurant, a family warming their hands by a fire in an oil barrel. This was not right.

2000: Failure and pivot

I left management consulting to join an internet start-up in San Francisco that, at the time, was merely a good idea with great potential. We raised over $70 million in venture funding, quickly grew to over 200 employees, and settled into a large warehouse complete with table tennis and the odd dog running around the cubicles. Later, I moved to London to manage our first client, ate all my meals out, and worked about eighty hours a week.

I was a mess. So was the business, and it failed after three years. This should not have been a surprise, given that 90% of all start-ups do fail. But I felt empty. I realized that I had pushed my life to the side to make this business succeed. With hindsight, I understood that this web services business did not necessarily hold any higher purpose for me. It was never going to address, let alone solve, some of the deeply entrenched issues – social injustice, climate crisis, poverty – that plague our society. So, I made a decision. The closing of my IT chapter created an opening to explore what a career in a more purpose-driven role could look like. I quickly filed for unemployment, packed my bags, and moved to Brussels to explore my options.

Many people have asked me why I chose to leave my life in the United States and move to a foreign country, with no job, no work permit, and plenty of student loan debt to pay off. The answer? Love. I had reconnected with the love of my life when I was based in London with the internet start-up and, having lost my job and decided to change careers, I had nothing to lose. It was a good choice. And I did eventually pay off my student loans.

2005: Crash and birth

My time in Brussels gave me the chance to pause and reflect. Where did I want to take my career? How could I integrate purpose into what I do? And where could I be most impactful? Through some creative networking (e.g., I flew to London to meet the Mozambique Country Director of a global NGO when he was in transit) and a bit of confidence building on my side, I landed a position to lead business development for the same organization in Mozambique.

After a short course in Portuguese, I flew to Maputo and began the second phase of my career: working on the frontlines to build small and growing businesses that create jobs and opportunities for Africans. My fiancé joined me a little later. My remit there was to help Mozambican entrepreneurs to build viable businesses in promising industries such as ecotourism, textiles, horticulture, and business process outsourcing.

While this was a fascinating challenge, I also felt a bit out of my comfort zone. Who was I to advise entrepreneurs in these sectors? Clearly, they knew more than I did. And that was true. But in the course of this work, I also learned that the value I could bring was in helping them achieve their full potential. This could be done, for example, by helping them access investment, linking them to markets, or even creating support groups to hone important skills. I loved the challenge of trying to do this, along with my team of smart Mozambican professionals, in a country I was just getting to know and a language I was just starting to speak. In the first few years, I also got married (to the same love of my life) and became pregnant with our first child.

And then I almost died

The trip itself was not particularly noteworthy. When I was six months pregnant, I traveled with a tourism expert and my team to the north of the country to meet with ecotourism operators. We were helping them connect to local communities to source fresh and local fruits and vegetables for their operations. This was the last trip I would take before my maternity leave and I was eager to make it a quick one, ideally without catching malaria in the process. It was a two-hour and thirty-minute flight from Maputo to Pemba, and then a short jump in a little Cessna Caravan plane over to Matemo Island. The island was being transformed into an ecotourism destination with a new resort, and we were going to explore how to make sure local communities benefited from this development.

But it didn't happen that way. On the approach, the plane impacted the ground before reaching the island's crude airstrip, losing its undercarriage, flipping over, and then bursting into flames. All I remember is silence. Deafening silence. And smoke. I was hanging upside down.

Seriously injured, the pilot scuttled out of the plane, shouting for us to do the same. All the others scooted out of the plane, except for me and one other, Eddie. I reached toward my seatbelt clasp and pulled. It did not open. My pregnant belly was hanging over it, and being upside down, I could not get the right angle to open it properly. I couldn't move.

Eddie, the tourism expert, was also still in the plane, but for different reasons. This was his second plane crash, and he didn't want to lose his laptop (and life's work) like he had in his inaugural plane crash. He was desperately searching for his bag.

Thanks to Eddie's bad luck with planes, I was able to get out of this one. He abandoned his mission to help me pry open my seatbelt clasp and support me, with my bulging belly, in navigating out of the plane. I couldn't look behind me, but I felt the heat of the fire as we half-ran, half-walked toward the hotel. The kind staff installed me in the honeymoon suite and brought fresh-squeezed pineapple juice. Later, once I was able to return home, doctors confirmed that my unborn child was not injured. But I still have a six-centimeter scar on my shoulder from the crash.

It took me a long time to talk about this experience. Seven years later, I shared the story in a TEDxZug talk, and I was surprised to discover how deeply it still impacts me. Perhaps this is because I never properly processed the trauma. I had quickly gone back to work and, three months later, had given birth to my first son, thus starting the whirlwind life of a full-time working mother.

But it did impact me by confirming the path that I chose that day in San Francisco when I packed up my things and booked a one-way ticket to Brussels. Life is short and precious. We must make careful choices about how to make the most of it.

2011: From receiving to giving

After nine years in Africa, I moved, with my family, to Europe to lead a private philanthropic foundation. This was the start of what would become the next phase in my 'purpose' career: building and growing three philanthropic foundations to tackle the most deeply rooted issues in our larger economic system. Specifically, I have been learning how to use this unique, risk-tolerant capital called philanthropy to catalyze a larger, systemic change. I am particularly excited by how philanthropy can both inspire and challenge business and industry to accelerate that change. For example, we used C&A Foundation's philanthropic capital to create Fashion for Good, an innovation accelerator that is now working with 12% of the global fashion industry to make fashion a force for good.

I also recognize that working in a foundation is a privileged position and, perhaps influenced by my near-decade of working in Africa, I have worked hard to make sure that we hold ourselves accountable for the impact we wish to have.

At the same time, I get impatient, if not a bit outraged. We are already in Year 4 of the Decisive Decade, and we are nowhere close to where we need to be to tackle the climate crisis. For that, we need to be bolder. Braver. We need to be willing to push aside our egos and individual needs for the benefit of the greater good – not just for us, the eight billion of us who are living, but for the 6.75 trillion who are yet to be born in the next 50,000 years (as many years as humans have lived so far). It's really for them that I do the work I do.

22 Relentless

Lisa Gautier[*]

The battle against climate change is everyone's responsibility, but not everyone can afford to care. I am about to take you through my story, what I care about, why I care about it, and why it means so much to me.

My name is Lisa Gautier, and I am what one might call a serial entrepreneur. Since 2010, I have joined, founded, and supported some of the most innovative companies in Europe.

I gained most of my insights from understanding how each company designs itself, scales, and communicates internally, and how one organization carries a single mission.

Originally from France, I have lived and worked across several European countries and tech hubs. From Berlin to Stockholm, and now in Zurich, I have always been motivated by absorbing insights from the highs and lows of innovation, technology, impact, and entrepreneurship.

This passion and drive led me to build and focus on developing my expertise and learning, experiencing as much as I could from small and large companies alike. I wish that I knew everything about everything, but because this is difficult indeed, I have chosen to specialize in the consumer space. From product development to leadership, from growth marketing to e-commerce, I have spent the past decade fueling myself with the most relevant growth topics of our time.

The fight

It was during my seven years in Stockholm that I became increasingly aware of the climate crisis and started to think of ways to use my knowledge to drive change toward sustainability. I was ready to take on a great fight.

---

[*] Serial Entrepreneur & Digital Growth Advisor

Unfortunately, and on a more personal level, I was fighting another difficult battle. My mother had been suffering for years from deteriorating mental health. Mental health is the kind of illness that leaves you with very little
direction and very little understanding of what to do and how much time
is *too much* time. This might be surprising to some people, but the more I
was exposed to the climate crisis, the more I became conflicted on how to
pick my battles. One was extremely personal and close to my heart, while
the other was affecting our entire world and potentially future generations.
This conflict made me feel that I could never do enough in either of those
battles. Eventually I became exhausted, felt constantly sad, and developed
a lot of anxiety.

Unfortunately, my mother ended up taking her own life. That day, nothing that I had accomplished in life mattered. None of it meant anything to
me anymore. This was probably one of the hardest times that I had to experience in my life. I needed to take time for and with my family, but I also knew
that something positive had to come out of this immense loss.

Fashion

Solving the climate crisis was one of the few things that still made sense. I
couldn't ignore the urgent need for change and turned a personal tragedy
into something positive. I needed to use all those years of hard work for
something meaningful.

Not everyone cares about the environment, for many reasons. I felt the
responsibility to care and commit. I had nothing stopping me, no excuses.
Politicians, decision-makers, executives, engineers – those who *can* care,
should care.

To me there are two types of 'for profit' impact companies: the long
shots, which require a lot of capital and a lot of research; and the ones optimizing for sustainability, that is, companies that can find immediate solutions in existing processes or behaviors.

In the second scenario, optimizing an existing behavior to make it in-
stantly more sustainable allows companies to create immediate, and hopefully scalable, impact.

I never thought that I could bring much value to companies that extract
CO2 from the air we breathe, or companies that build enormous plants to
turn by-products into pulp and other innovative materials.

Rather, my mission, the one I carry to this day, is to reshape one of the
most polluting industries on earth: fashion. A lot of people believe that we
need to educate consumers in buying higher-quality garments and to invest
in longer-lasting items. This is true, but it is also unrealistic. The majority

of consumers don't have the means to buy a t-shirt for $100. Because some people are simply trying to make ends meet, it's very unlikely that sustainability will reach the top of their priority list. Meanwhile, they're likely to account for most of the low-cost commodities that are produced every day.

In my work, I want to create sustainable options for them by building solutions that fit their budget and helping them make changes to their needs and lifestyles. Looking at it another way, companies such as Beyond Burger weren't created to convince vegetarians to eat less meat. They were designed to provide a tasty alternative to meat for meat eaters.

My vision is to create an alternative to fast fashion that provides the exact same level of satisfaction without sacrificing the appeal of instant gratification. It's a solution that requires no compromises and turns harmful habits into sustainable ones – something that puts both consumers and manufacturers on a path to a fully circular economy. My definition of success is a business that combines exponential growth with a global impact. It's a business that shows profitability and inspires both investors and founders to invest their resources in the environmental challenges that we all face.

It was in 2019 that I took my shot, launching hackyourcloset.com (HYC). In this, I collaborated with a contact of mine working in a VC firm who shared my goal of reducing the fashion industry's devastating footprint. We looked at many emerging circular business models, combined our ideas, and brainstormed on several occasions. In just a few weeks, I launched an MVP (minimal viable product), acquired our first customers, and started growing revenue.

Hackyourcloset.com was a consumer service that shipped a monthly curated selection of clothes to subscribers. For only EUR 29.90 per month, our 3000 customers were able to borrow garments and get access to new options monthly. Using exclusively unsold items, overstocks, and second-hand garments, our mission was to maximize their value and significantly reduce their climate footprint.

Our data-driven and proprietary technology allowed us to optimize the use of our clothes across all customers. After just a year, we became a proven positive impact enabler and became Life Cycle Assessment certified. We contributed to the renowned Ellen MacArthur Foundation's research on circular business models and participated in the European Commission for circular economy.

In less than two years, we achieved EUR 1.4 million in recurring revenues, rescued over 70,000 garments from the waste stream, reduced our subscribers' clothes consumption footprint by 97%, grew to forty employees, and raised close to $ 3million. HYC was the leading player in its field, by far.

Rebirth

Sadly, the world had other plans. A global pandemic, a war, and an economic downturn forced my co-founder, our team, and me to make a tough decision. In July 2022, we closed the company, not as an act of surrender but as a strategic move to preserve our drive, achievements, and expertise. It was time to give back to our team and give them the opportunity to rethink their career paths and seek opportunities before the looming recession. The aim was for us to see how the situation would evolve, wait for conditions to stabilize, and hopefully one day pick up right where we left off.

To create a sustainable future, we must identify our individual contributions, learn from our failures, and adapt quickly. The road ahead may require taking three steps forward and two steps back, but we must persevere. We can never give up. Though my journey has been far from linear, I will always remain committed to the environment.

Today, I work as a senior digital strategy consultant for a leading B-Corp certified technology and marketing agency. I continue to learn and grow, getting my inspiration from those who have succeeded while reflecting on what I could have done better. In the end, it's not about how far we've come or how much we've achieved. It's about the relentless pursuit of a better world and the profound realization that, together, we can create the change we so desperately need.

23   What a wonderful world

Manilla Calabrese[*]

I work as an architect. When I graduated from the University of Turin, at the turn of the millennium, I did so with a host of environmentalist dreams about energy-saving buildings.

But I also understood the reality: that buildings 'boast' the highest pollution and energy consumption rates of any type of activity after factories, not only during construction but also in operation. My ideal of an avant-garde architecture involved the intelligent application of the most advanced technologies to *remotely* perform all activities that do not require social interaction and to experience, *live and together*, the spaces of an unseen world. For me, this represents a delicately inhabited nature where technology would be invisible and magical.

The opposite is happening. Today, we remotely perform activities that require sociality, and we often live in solitude in anthills of asphalt, concrete, and iron.

Micro-scaling

My ideal project starts from the micro-scale, aware that the outside – the macro-scale, the world – is the inescapable mirror of our own interiority. This project focuses on self-work, on the precision and nonviolence of communication, on educating people on things that are beautiful and good, and on creating a community that lives by these values.

The starting community, in this magical project, is connected to a network of other living communities, aimed at concretely experiencing authentic and connected living and dwelling.

[*] Architect

Now, I am pursuing the search for a disused village – one that is immersed in nature and full of vital energy. And it must have all the characteristics of a village: small dimensions, contextualized architecture in terms of form and materials, the presence of clearings for cultivation, and the presence of abundant sunshine and spring water. The 'dream' is to snatch this village from decadence and to create the prototype of another true earth on the earth we already inhabit. This requires that economy, education, politics, social organization, science, medicine, art, and education are pursued clearly and freely – free of the interests of the few, and free from the mistakes of the past.

In this formulation, a new planet earth – a new way of living *on* our planet – can only arise when we work on creating new values, putting aside our egos and reconnecting with nature – and people – as a whole, as an integrated community. We must work from the heart and not always from the mind. Only in this way can we imagine a new and different world from the ground up.

Harmony

Back in my university days, the relation between constructions and the environment was something of a sticking point. I had found in the library all the books related to the theme of dear old ecology – today renamed with the anglophone terms 'green' and 'sustainability' – which have their roots in bioclimatic, feng shui, natural architecture, and organicism. I devoured techniques and technologies of the symbiosis between architecture and the environment, eager for knowledge. It seemed far-fetched to me that the dissonance between inhabitant and inhabited planet was due to mankind, while the entire animal world teaches us how to integrate *with* the planet.

From this, the 'dream of the new world' took the form of a 'return': to ancient knowledge, to the laws of physics, to respect for orography, hydrography, vegetation, to the simple and the small, to common sense. All roads seemed to lead to Rome. And Rome was the contextualization of solutions, the skillful use of local materials, the study of the site, and the understanding of the *genius loci*, the spirit and the 'needs' of the place (it is no coincidence that igloos are not made of bricks) – in short, the antithesis of blanket, pre-packaged solutions.

But why do I do it? Because, today, there is no alternative.

Doing *business with* planet earth means trying to profit from the natural cycles of the elements: water, air, earth. It is like producing bottles of clean air with polluting processes and selling them at a high price. The environment cannot be a plus-value, a luxury. Living in tune with natural cycles should be a prerequisite and a necessity, and we should adapt ourselves intelligently *to* our environment.

It can be argued that the situation we are confronted with is perilous, and that all that can be done is to implement virtuous business models that seek to reverse and correct this disastrous trend. And this is true, at least in part. But meaningful models can only be generated by people who are aware of the natural world and not unconscious of it. As Einstein argued, "A problem cannot be solved with the same mindset that generated it." To achieve this we must desire it, replacing hope with proactivity.

Action

The first route we must pursue is related to holography. It starts with *me*, knowing I am who I say I am. I must work on my 'inner garden' and reflect on the beauty of the outside world. The holographic universe sees the 'whole' in its smallest fragment. What image is closer to this physical law than a drop of water in the sea? In my professional practice, individual actions come first. I reuse my waste as much as possible, including it even in my creative design. I reuse washing water for domestic drains and for the irrigation of my plants. These plants in turn provide the crops and vegetables that I eat, only supplementing them with the produce of a small local farm. I optimize car journeys on medium-long distances by offering rides and, when working from home, I reduce the absolute number of journeys I make. Where I can, I choose materials that are natural, 'alive,' and changeable. I have a sober lifestyle, in contact with nature, in the mountains and the vegetable garden. Before talking about hierarchical levels, national and international and global, one must start with oneself, the individual.

My second route concerns concreteness, integrity, and responsibility. "It is you from the city who call it nature: it is so abstract in your head that even the name is abstract. We, here, say forest, pasture, stream, rock, things one can point to with one's finger. Things that can be used. If they can't be used, we don't give them a name because it's useless." So says Bruno the mountain man in the movie *The Eight Mountains* (2022).

We don't respect the law of gravity. We experience it. If I strip a land of trees, it dries up. If I pollute water, I cannot drink it. If I burn plastic, it stinks and blackens the air. Using abstract conceptual categories – such as 'environment,' 'strategies,' and 'green' – distances us from our responsibility. If I say 'environment,' I may not take care of my garden because I do not identify it with the environment. My own life, although I live in a metropolis, is steeped in the 'environment,' from the balcony on which I find other people's cigarette butts to the overpass I walk under that is full of rubbish.

My third route relates to simplicity. The first method of waste reduction does not make use of some sophisticated annihilation technology but consists in not producing things in the first place. Bioclimatic architecture acts upstream, directly on form and material, on orientation and on non-energy-consuming energy supply devices. Think of the ventilation chimneys of Mediterranean countries, which naturally extract warm air from houses by exploiting the thermal inertia of the earth – in defiance of any super-efficient air conditioning system. The Climate House protocol, for example, reverses the traditional concept of reducing system consumption because it aims to eliminate it altogether through good insulation and an energy-efficient building envelope. The problem must be revolutionized. That is, we must not ask ourselves how we can make a heating system that is more efficient but challenge the actual *need* for it. Put more simply still: "Do I need this?"

My fourth route relates to unity and spirit. I 'am' my environment. If I feel connected to my environment, I do not need to respect it because it is no one other than me. In short, it is a matter of connection between the inner environment of humanity and the 'seemingly' outer place of the environment we inhabit. The 'environmental question' is first and foremost spiritual. It is not about money, investment, technology, or politics. It is about making humanity and earth one. But I am not just talking about metaphysics and invisible energies. Are the chemical elements and the laws that govern them different? Carbon, hydrogen, oxygen. If we are 'children of the stars,' it is not only by poetic license, but also by analogy of substance.

We are one.

24 Can we save our planet, one rhymed story at a time?

Mara Catherine Harvey[*]

Our world is in trouble: our planet is sick!
There are some big problems we really must fix.
We must find a balance in all that we do,
so nature can flourish, and people can, too.
What is it exactly that needs to be done?
Could finding this balance be something fun?
Can you save the planet if you're just a kid?
I'd say: Yes, indeed! It's high time we all did!

I had never planned to become a children's book author, let alone an advocate for the United Nations' seventeen Sustainable Development Goals (SDGs). It all happened quite serendipitously, as so many things in life do. Six years ago, I held a keynote at a conference in Zurich and at the end of it, I was handed a bag with a "Dream. Dare. Do." notebook and a card that said: "What would you do if you weren't afraid?"

It was such a simple question and yet so hard to answer. It took me a day or two. If I could do anything I wanted, without fear or constraint, what would I do? The answer I barely dared to whisper to myself was Ambassador for the United Nations.

I really must put this into context. I am an economist by background and a banker by profession; I have worked for over twenty years in wealth management. Very little of what I do daily has to do with saving the planet. And yet everything I deal with every day has a massive impact on our world. So, allow me to rewind a little further, to explain what brought me to where I am today.

----

[*] CEO VP Bank Switzerland & Head Region Europe

Money and women

If there is one thing that was blatantly missing in the world of finance throughout my career, it was women. Not just women in senior management positions; female wealth management clients were few and far between, too. I knew that in the developing world women were invisible to the financial system because they were largely unbanked. But it seemed such a paradox that even in developed countries, women were largely invisible to the financial industry, too. They were largely ignored and were underserved. Even worse, many women were caught in a 'safety trap,' believing they didn't have enough money to start investing and could not afford to take risks by doing so.

Researching women's attitudes toward money was what made me a financial feminist and led me to author *Women and Risk: Rewriting the Rules* (Nicolai Intelligence & Publishing, Berlin, 2018). After sizing up the impact over a lifetime of taking – or not taking – full control of your finances, I knew I needed to act. Alongside my day job, I spent every minute of my free time, nights, weekends, and holidays, doing more research and advocacy to increase female financial participation and spark industry-wide debate. This was only the beginning of my journey from gender equality in finance to advocacy for the seventeen SDGs.

You know that nagging feeling when you're missing something but you're not quite sure what? That feeling accompanied me every day. While I was appealing to adult women to take control of their financial future, I was wondering why women engage differently than men do when it comes to discussing money. The penny finally dropped when I stumbled upon research that showed that pay gaps are already visible in children's pocket money. Unbelievable but true.

Filling the gap

This was the fabulous rabbit hole I fell into, like Alice in Wonderland. Pay gaps. Wealth gaps. Pension gaps. Money habits. Money mindsets. Gender gaps. Root causes. Pocket money. Kids. Parents. These notions were just whirling around in my mind. I knew this had so many ramifications, but I couldn't put my finger on them all just yet. I was curious to know how deep the rabbit hole was.

When are money habits formed? What determines a person's financial capability? How is money knowledge acquired? How are money skills formed? What influences a person's money attitudes? How are money behaviors shaped? What boosts or hinders a child's confidence in talking about and dealing with money? And finally, what role does gender play in all this? There were so many questions I needed answers to.

Finding these answers led to many more questions. I was far from having reached the bottom of the rabbit hole. Why do girls ask for less? Why is their work valued less? When is it that children's innate sense of fairness is erased and replaced with the notions of competition, power, and greed that we traditionally associate with money? And what if we could change that, too? Could we teach kids about money in a way that not only empowers them to take control of their financial future but also empowers them to take care of our environmental future? What if we could teach children that money goes hand in hand with empowerment, equality, and environmental care? Because every single one of our daily money decisions has an impact on our world.

Crash landing. I had reached the bottom and here I stood. It had all come full circle. I realized that everything I was dealing with every single day as a wealth manager had the power of positive impact, well beyond notions of ESG investing. Money truly could become a force for good if we could overcome our outdated money beliefs anchored in power and greed. Naively optimistic, I felt, and still feel, that we can collectively shift our money mindsets if we can rethink the way we introduce money to children.

Kids' stuff

Money is not just a transmission of value. It's a transmission of values. This is so simple, yet borderline impossible. I set out to create a new money learning journey for children and to enable parents to introduce money much more mindfully to their children by identifying learning objectives in terms of skills, values, and confidence-building blocks; defining clear financial parenting principles; establishing a systematic framework for money and ethics to go hand in hand; and laying out simple steps to introduce pocket money and the positive values we would like children to associate with money.

At first, I got many puzzled looks when I told people I had written a children's book on earning and equal pay. This wasn't deemed an appropriate topic for five- to seven-year-olds. It still takes a lot of explaining. Yet shouldn't we start by teaching children where money comes from, and that this is where fairness plays a crucial role – for each one of us and for society's future?

Then, of course, kids need to learn all about saving, patience, and delayed gratification; about spending and prioritizing wisely; about digital money and planning and tracking; and, most importantly, about spending choices and their impact on our planet. Finally (the part that should come first, as Simon Sinek so rightly says), there is the core of the learning journey: *Why* our money choices are so important! Our planet has seventeen problems we need to resolve: the seventeen SDGs. My mission is for every child to learn their SDGs like their ABCs, so they know why every money choice they will make in life matters so much.

When people ask me: why books and not a gaming app for kids? Isn't this old fashioned? My answer is simple. Research shows that reading out loud to and with your child helps them develop not only their social and emotional skills, but also their executive functioning skills. In short, the latter are essential for self-management and delaying gratification – two essential skills for good money and impact management over a lifetime.

Slow finance

In today's world, we don't take time for this. We plant our kids in front of devices and let them consume content, alone. We assume they are learning all about money by playing with apps that offer virtual or digital money, plus instant gratification to keep kids in-app. Meanwhile, our own daily interactions with money have become a swipe or a tap: money is merely an action in the eyes of our small children and is no longer seen as a transaction (we don't give away our phone or card to execute a payment, and children below age seven don't yet understand the abstract concept of a digital money transfer).

This 'fast finance' is like 'fast food.' You wouldn't feed your child fast food every day and assume they are growing up with a healthy diet. So why do we think that feeding a child fast finance every day will offer them healthy money habits?

Mine is a plea for 'slow finance,' to raise financially capable kids who truly master the money skills they need for life before unleashing them in a digital world that is luring them into consumerism. My books on money are a tool for this slow finance journey. Making time for meaningful money conversations and role modeling money in front of children (financial parenting) are the other essential ingredients for parents to master this journey. It is so easy, and yet so hard. Intentionality is key.

Intentionality is at the heart of my learning journey for children and parents. The best part? The children's books are all in rhymes! It's not by chance, it's by design. Rhymes are fun and they stick with us for life. We never forget those nursery rhymes we grew up with when we were little. Isn't that the best possible way to ensure a child will never forget the very first values they associate with money? I think it is, but I'll leave it to you and your children to judge, over the decades and generations to come.

No child ever should be poor,
nor be hungry ever more.
Nor be ill without good care,
so, life is better everywhere.

Children need to go to school,
and equal treatment is the rule.
Everywhere you go you'd see
clean water and clean energy.

With decent jobs, life's more fun,
so, growth is good for everyone!
Infrastructure is the key
to lower inequality.

We must build sustainably
our cities and communities.
Spending wisely when we buy,
means our planet will not die.

Save the oceans and the seas,
the animals and all the trees.
For the world to live in peace,
let's all be good partners please!

"Start Doing Good (SDG)" explains in rhymes the seventeen SDGs to children ages five to ten years. It has been published in the United Nations library and is free for all to read. It is the fifth book of the Smart Way to Start book series on money and ethics for children.

25 My life, my world

Maria Vincenza Chiriacò[*]

It all started on a spring morning at primary school, at the age of ten, when our teacher came into the classroom railing against the tree pruning that was going on outside. As dozens of workers pruned the long row of trees, she explained to us that the vegetative period of those trees had just started after the long winter period of rest, which would have been the right time to prune them. Instead, the trees were suffering: all the sap and energy that had been dedicated to producing new leaves, flowers, and fruits would be redirected to closing the wounds caused by the cuts, which would alter the trees' biological cycle.

That was when I first understood the unique and interconnected role that trees and plants play on our planet.

My classmates and I were captivated by what our teacher told us and wanted to do something to stop the trees' suffering. We spent the morning writing essays arguing the importance of properly managing urban green areas. Our teacher collated our responses into one essay and shared it with the local newspaper, which published it for the whole city to read. We were praised as the children who took a stand to defend the trees.

Since that day, my interest in plant ecosystems and the intricacies of the climate emergency and anthropomorphic climate change has grown. In 2010, I secured a research doctorate in Forest Sciences and mastered in Climate Change. My PhD thesis aimed to develop a method to calculate how much CO_2 trees in urban and rural areas could capture and store, and thus contribute to climate change mitigation.

[*] Co-Director of the Division on Climate Change Impacts on Agriculture, Forests and Ecosystem Services, CMCC Foundation

Trees will save us

Enhancing trees' and vegetative ecosystems' capacity to mitigate climate change is my main goal. Greenhouse gas emissions have reached unprecedented levels and the effects in terms of climate change are now being felt by us all; the destruction caused by extreme floods and summer wildfires make regular headlines, and our food systems and agricultural production are buckling under the stress of rising temperatures and prolonged drought.

According to the IPCC, if we reach global net zero emissions by the end of this century the increase in the average temperature of the planet will be contained under 2°C compared with pre-industrial levels. Beyond that threshold, humanity won't be able to adapt to the changed conditions: our agricultural systems won't be able to provide enough food for everyone, the temperatures in our cities will reach inhospitable highs, and we will see entire ecosystems destroyed.

A drastic reduction in GHG emissions can be achieved if all countries put in place joint efforts in various sectors, from energy that must become 100% renewable, to agriculture, industry, and transport. But the ambitious goal of climate neutrality can only be achieved by leveraging the unique capacity of our natural ecosystems to absorb CO_2 from the atmosphere. At the European level, projections tell us that at a certain point in the reduction journey, GHG emissions will be hard to abate, and natural carbon sinks will play a crucial role in reaching and achieving Europe's 2050 carbon neutrality target. By maintaining and planting forests and green spaces, the European Union can improve carbon sequestration capacity, reduce air pollution, and regulate temperature in cities while preserving vital plant and animal species.

As co-director of the Division on Impacts of Climate Change on Agriculture, Forests and Ecosystem Services at CMCC (Euro-Mediterranean Center on Climate Change) I spend my time aiming to understand how to measure, protect, and enhance this unique ability of plants to contribute to climate change mitigation by sequestering CO_2 from the atmosphere.

Since 2010, there have been many projects that I have followed, conceived, developed, and coordinated with colleagues and partners across Europe and beyond. They have involved studying the effects of sustainable forest and agricultural management practices on the global carbon balance, the development of decision support systems for policymakers and farmers, assessing the impact of our food choices, and designing virtuous mechanisms to reduce emissions and increase carbon removals, such as schemes for carbon farming and voluntary carbon markets.

One of my current projects focuses on building an understanding of how to regenerate the landscape and agriculture of Salento, Italy, a land that is dear to me and where my family origins are. In southernmost Puglia, at Italy's heel, this region is historically characterized by its ancient olive trees, which are being threatened by the *xylella fastidiosa* bacterium that has killed more than 21 million trees and reduced the region's status as the country's prime olive oil producer. To help with the regeneration of this land, we are building a tool that can help farmers and policymakers understand which plant species are suitable replacements for the dead olive trees, with the aim to increase biodiversity and differentiate the landscape to build its resilience to the expected impacts of climate change and to help create more natural carbon sinks.

In another ambitious European project that I coordinate, SWITCH (2023–2026), twenty partners from eight different European countries are working together to set up practical actions to help farmers, food producers, and consumers understand how important it is for us and for the planet to reduce emissions from agricultural production and to adopt a healthy and sustainable diet.

That's life

Outside of work, my personal life is oriented toward sustainability, and I try to reduce my impact every day. I live in the historic center of Viterbo, the city where I work, in an ancient stone house that we restored using only wood and natural materials. I try to make conscious lifestyle and food choices and educate my daughter in the full respect of our planet. And the organic and sustainable farm Trebotti that my husband runs on the hills that dominate the Teverina valley at the border between Lazio, Tuscany and Umbria is often our open lab where I measure and test solutions. He is on the frontline of the climate emergency, facing its effects on his produce. He strains to produce high-quality wines from local varieties with the least impact possible on the environment and the landscape where we spend a great part of our free time. On the farm, I have been measuring GHG emissions and fluxes, assessing the capacity of sustainable agricultural production to mitigate climate change and the impacts the vines suffer, and testing new solutions such as innovative sensors. Many of these results are also published as scientific papers with the aim to share solutions and inspire other researchers and farmers.

The farm is an example and a reference point for sustainable agricultural production. It frequently wins awards for its commitment to sustainable production, hosts many students to learn and practice on climate change and sustainable agriculture, and receives thousands of ecotourists every year who are eager to know a true story of sustainable rurality.

I firmly believe in the work that scientists and politicians must do to find solutions and apply them in the most efficient way, but beyond this, even the small daily choices of each of us are fundamental to achieving big changes.

26 CEO and Board journey from compliance to courage

Marina Cvetkovic & Nicole Heimann[*]

With the business sector contributing roughly 70% of the GDP in OECD markets, there is a consensus that the corporate leadership, that is, CEOs, executive teams, and boards, play a tremendously important role in creating a better today and tomorrow for everyone. Our society has been trying hard to move the needle of awareness on these levels for more than a decade – unfortunately, with very limited success.

Because of the urgency and severity of multiple ESG matters, society – governments, non-governmental bodies, shareholders, and other stakeholders – have tended to impose more and more ESG regulations and requirements upon the business sector. While many organizations are attempting to meet at least some of the requirements, it is often done with the single goal to appease the governments and activists, rather than to truly move the needle on the burning ESG issues themselves.

This is the so-called compliance mindset, well known in the psychology literature, which emphasizes the containment of wrongdoing and adherence to rules – that is, meeting the (minimum) requirements for compliance's sake only. As a result, despite good intentions and significant investment, many companies are falling short. Their commitments are not bold enough. Their efforts are disconnected and incremental.

As co-CEOs of an award-winning executive advisory firm based out of Zurich and New York, we decided to join this critically important movement as CEO advisors and coaches. Our approach to helping CEOs rise to this pressing challenge is radically different from that of any other constituents. We have become intimately familiar with the workings of the human brain and understand that the key to a breakthrough in the ESG space is breaking out of the compliance mindset. The world needs CEOs and boards who are marching full speed, not only to meet externally imposed

[*] Founders & CEOs of Heimann Cvetkovic & Partners

ESG targets and requirements, but who courageously lead efforts that go way beyond that. In other words, the only way to truly move the needle is to elevate the level of consciousness of the executives in charge of the business sector to a level where leading courageously, leading for tomorrow, leading across the ecosystem becomes their only possible way of operating. Beyond the leadership actions of decarbonizing and creating net zero companies and meeting ESG targets, CEOs must dramatically shift their leadership style and mindset. This applies not only to the CEOs but also the boards, the executive teams, and ultimately all employees and stakeholders too. How the leadership alliance between the board, the CEO, and the executive team works is directly reflected across the organization and, of course, in the results of the company.

Elevating consciousness is a complex undertaking, much more complex than throwing a few metrics at someone and occasionally checking to see if they are complying. It requires collective work at a much deeper level than the level on which we have had this conversation so far. To create a new world, moon shots at the top are necessary. As Albert Einstein famously said: "We cannot solve our problems with the same level of thinking that created them." CEOs need to unlearn what they were taught was right for years and relearn what is needed to create a new world.

In working with many CEOs, leadership teams, and boards in recent years, we identified three big waves of transformation through which CEOs and boards experience the deep shifts that are necessary on their journey toward courageous and regenerative leadership.

Wave 1: Letting go of ego

To shift leaders from compliance to courage, the most basic and most difficult mindset change that is needed at the deepest level is the ability to let go of ego. The revolution for a better tomorrow needs leaders who are truly, authentically in it not just for themselves. It takes leaders who have either done the self-work or are willing to do it, to become fully aware of the ego part of themselves – the part that is always looking for more power and external recognition – and learn how to keep it at bay. It takes leaders who are connected to their purpose and their authentic selves, and who don't need to be recognized as 'heroes' for every effort they make in creating a better future for everyone.

We need leaders who are so driven by their own sense of purpose and service to the world that compliance alone could never possibly be the point at which their efforts stop. They must have an abundant mindset and not be concerned that giving more would ever lead to them having less – they must know that on this journey, the more each one of us gives, the more we will all receive in return.

Wave 2: Working together beyond ego

As leaders let go of their ego, the next wave on this transformational journey of leading regeneratively is starting to see the world around them differently. Suddenly, the narrative "Me against them" (activists, board, regulatory bodies, etc.) is gone, and a leader who previously might have been defensive, ignorant, or, at best, mildly engaged starts feeling a much stronger connection to the matters at hand. He or she starts to feel the inherent 'oneness' of the universe and to view their employees, partners, regulators, shareholders, but also the society as a whole, and nature, very differently.

As truly regenerative leaders, CEOs unlearn the anthropocentric or egocentric view of the world in which humans are deemed more important than other living beings and relearn an ecocentric view of the world in which the wellbeing of the earth and nature is deemed more important and critical to the survival of our planet. They can consider both the short-term expectations of shareholders and the long-term impact their decisions today will have on the next generations.

As they let go of their ego and connect to their core sense of purpose, they essentially connect to the love in them. Love is often seen as taboo in corporate environments, relegated to a mere emotion that belongs in our intimate spheres. But as new generations demand more of their leaders, challenging them to think beyond profit and growth, love is finding its way back into the workplace. A leader connected to their heart makes decisions differently. With the best interest of their employees and the world at large in mind, they may shift away from a mindset that is result- and profit-driven only. As Duncan Coombe found in his research, "love is the underlying impulse behind corporate citizenship and sustainability." A natural attribute that comes with love is the desire to protect. And if you do not love nature, why would you protect it?

Wave 3: Leading the ecosystem

The last wave on the transformational journey of regenerative leadership is usually the most visible one to the external world. This is the phase when CEOs start to take bold action from a place of a radically changed mindset. They start taking a stand on the most pressing matters facing society and they fully assume their share of the responsibility to create a better tomorrow. They come up with innovative and creative ideas to align purpose, profit, and productivity in a way that lifts all constituents higher. They start embracing and initiating alliances with everyone, including their competitors, partners, and suppliers, as they understand that ESG challenges can only be resolved together. In their shift from compliance to courage, CEOs even transform their relationship with their board, finding new ways to truly leverage it as a strategic asset in the joint ESG effort. Instead of leading just their own organization, they step up to leading entire ecosystems that stretch way beyond their company walls.

The challenge today is the disconnect between the bold action society demands from CEOs on the one hand, and the incremental progress most of them are making on the other hand. The issue is quite simple at the core: CEOs are only humans, with their own sets of limitations. Before they overcome them, they simply will not be able to step up in the way that is needed. Most CEOs are simply not able to execute on courageous deeds because the deeper work of transcending the ego as well as the mindset shifts that would need to precede such action have not taken place.

Focus

This is why we devote our time exclusively to a select number of courageous CEOs, helping them transcend the ego and achieve the mindset shifts related to the three transformational waves of regenerative leadership to unlock their full potential to become a powerful force for good. We are committed to work only with leaders who understand that they can be extraordinary multipliers and who are willing to do the work needed to do so. These are the CEOs who are also super-connectors in the broader ecosystem and responsibly manage the shadow they cast. Working together as a CEO advisory team, we focus on the impact CEOs want to create, the growth they aspire to, and the legacy they want to leave.

27 The power of will

Marina Nitsa Viergutz[*]

I was born and raised in Ukraine, in the beautiful town of Odessa by the Black Sea. As a child, I felt the challenges of life under Soviet rule, and the subsequent chaos that followed its dissolution. From those less-than-ideal formative years, to the current unjustifiable struggles brought upon my compatriots, the story of Ukraine gives me motivation, inspiration, and energy to work toward a more perfect world. I learned to be grateful for what I have, but always to push for others to have a fair share as well.

My parents are my other key source of inspiration. Their decision to move our family from Ukraine to the United States when I was a teenager was not driven by economic hardship, discrimination, or the like but rather by an unexpected opportunity that they chose to pursue. This courageous decision, to leave a relatively comfortable life and step into the unknown, continues to drive me toward fresh challenges.

The dream

Once I arrived in the United States, I strived for the 'American Dream.' At the age of twenty, while my college classmates were enjoying campus life, I took on a job at a boutique investment bank where I worked full time while pursuing double major degrees in Accounting and Finance. I was also very interested in global affairs and did two study abroad missions, one in China and another in India, both of which were eye-opening experiences that left deep impressions.

After gaining professional experience at the bank, I made the decision to continue my career in finance and joined JPMorgan's analyst program in New York. After four rewarding years there, I followed the traditional

---

[*] Partner, Arieli Capital

banker's path and went on to get an MBA. I then joined Credit Suisse's Alternative Investment team, first in Switzerland and then in Singapore. In my last role there, I oversaw a multibillion-dollar hedge fund business in Asia and was leading private equity distribution efforts for key Southeast Asian markets.

Since 2019, I switched my focus to VC, investing in early-stage technology companies and innovation platforms globally. I am not just an investor, but also a hands-on operator, and I get involved with portfolio companies to help them execute on business plans, which we often define together.

Life

The work–life balance has never been my strength and I tend to immerse myself in work. However, I am fortunate to have the opportunity to work on meaningful projects and create real impact in my day-to-day job. In my spare time, I dedicate time to my family, which is certainly the most important and rewarding part of my life. Maintaining the right balance between work and life is never easy; it requires constant prioritization to ensure one doesn't benefit to the detriment of the other. The only time I allow myself to be away from family is for sports or volunteering and I hope that, as my children get older, we can enjoy these activities together.

I believe that athletic pursuits allow me to stay focused and productive. If that means waking up at 5 am to squeeze in a quick workout before a busy day, I will do it. Last year I ran a marathon, which was a great challenge. It was mind over matter for me, as I didn't have the time to train properly, resulting in a rather challenging second half. When I hit that metaphorical wall and felt like I really couldn't continue, I told myself that it was all in my head and pushed myself to complete the challenge.

That rewarding experience was a reminder that, when things get hard, in sports or life, everything is possible with focus and determination. One can frequently find me at fitness studios or outdoors playing tennis, jogging, or skiing. Frankly, if someone wants to hang out with me, there's a good chance I will invite them to play sports together or try to recruit them for one of my volunteer activities.

Giving back

On the volunteer front, I leverage my now nearly twenty-year professional expertise working with leading financial institutions and investment boutiques across the United States, Europe, and Asia to help start-ups and non-profit organizations. I'm an avid supporter of the start-up community and contribute enthusiastically to VC ecosystem building. I mentor start-ups across multiple organizations such as Seedstars and Founders Institute, among others. I'm focused on founders in emerging markets, mission-driven companies, and those run by minorities.

I am also passionate about supporting the next generation of leaders with a particular focus on women and other underrepresented communities. I have held several leadership positions within the 100 Women in Finance organization and CFA Society. Within these groups, I have organized and led multiple discussions with industry leaders, such as conversations with Stephanie Cohen from Goldman Sachs and many other world-class leaders. Recently, I led a discussion on Women Entrepreneurship in Zurich, with two inspiring entrepreneurs who shared practical advice on how to start, operate, and exit a business. I have also collaborated closely with a Swiss FinTech company that is made of female investors, and where I currently serve as an ambassador.

I have also engaged with several non-profits. When I lived in Singapore I collaborated with Aidha organization, which offers education to foreign domestic workers who often have very limited resources, have limited education, and come to wealthier countries (e.g., Singapore, Dubai, and others) to work long hours for little pay. I worked with the organization's CEO to create a new learning module in their curricula on financial literacy and insurance.

When I lived in Chicago, I dedicated time to the Chicago Grants association, which is focused on offering financial support to companies that serve underrepresented communities in troubled neighborhoods of Chicago. I was primarily focused on assessing their financial strength and the impact they create for the purpose of selecting grant winners.

On the professional front, I try to get involved in projects that are disruptive and create impact. A few years ago I was on the board of an early-stage company that enables underserved and underprivileged individuals to obtain savings and investment solutions, as well as life insurance. Projects such as these give me satisfaction as I see the real impact they have on people's livelihoods.

Impact

In my current role as a Partner at Arieli Capital, I am particularly proud of the high-impact projects that our firm is involved in. Our portfolio companies include those that address autoimmune diseases (which primarily impact women), infertility treatments, and a platform that supports new parents. That is not even mentioning the numerous charitable organizations that we partner with.

One effort worth highlighting is Frontier, an investment and partnership between Arieli Capital and the Ramat Hanegev Research and Development Center in Israel's Negev highlands. This project focuses on the challenges of how to feed a rapidly growing population while mitigating the impacts of climate change. In many parts of the world, farmers are struggling with droughts, heat waves, and other extreme weather events that are becoming more frequent and intense due to global warming. Amid this growing crisis, some innovators and entrepreneurs are developing new technologies and business models to transform agriculture and secure our future food supply. The region where Frontier is situated is known for its harsh, desert-like conditions and extreme climate, making it a challenging environment for agriculture. Yet Ramat Hanegev has been at the forefront of agricultural innovation for the past seventy years, developing ground-breaking protocols and technologies to grow crops in these difficult conditions. Today, Ramat Hanegev produces a wide variety of crops, including olives, grapes, pineapples, and even strawberries, all in conditions that would be considered impossible in most other parts of the world. They also produce 95% of Israel's renewable energy and provide a beta site for five agri-voltaic start-ups.

Venture capital and innovation through technological advancement is the way to make a real impact, and Frontier is doing just that. Their mission is to connect select agri-tech start-ups with the real-world assets they need to succeed. This includes direct connections to farmers, access to farmland, world-renowned researchers, grants, and beta sites. Combined with the expertise of Arieli Capital in global business development, opening new markets, and investments, Frontier is uniquely positioned to help start-ups secure scalable solutions for humanity's food crisis.

I am proud of what we are achieving there and look forward to being involved not only with Frontier, but also with many other projects that advance the goal of tackling climate change, a truly existential threat to us all.

28 Defining a legacy

Marisa Drew[*]

A couple of years ago, a chief executive I worked with asked me a rather profound question: "What do you want your legacy to be?"

As an investment banker, that question is not normally at the front of the mind as we always have an eye on the next deal, but it got me thinking. What if I could use my long tenure in investment banking and capital markets experience – all those years of structuring transactions and raising capital – for something that could make a real difference to the world and to the generation that comes after me? I thought, what a great opportunity as the next step in the twilight of a long career.

Having worked in the realm of traditional finance for thirty years, the risk this question brought into focus was that I would plateau in my learning, skills development, and contribution if I carried on in a linear pathway. Up to that point, however, combining purpose and profit in the form of sustainability had not presented itself as being a strategic career option. It wasn't until that fateful conversation that I deliberately pivoted my career trajectory and began a whole new learning journey.

Since 2017, embracing the business side of sustainability has become not only strategically important for the future of the finance industry but also a prerequisite. This might seem like a given today, but at that time, it was quite a new concept for a P&L (profit and loss) responsible banker. What was intriguing for me, in effect the 'hook' that attracted me to consider this as a next step in my career, was the role I could play as a frontline banker in tangibly contributing to the evolution of the financial sector and the betterment of society at the same time. Initially I was somewhat suspect that this was possible, but my CEO challenged me as a starting point to do some due diligence and meet the thought leaders and innovators already making an

---

[*] Chief Sustainability Officer, Standard Chartered

impact in the ecosystem. That really opened my eyes to what this opportunity could become.

I have no doubt that the world is changing for the better. In those early days of exploring, I wasn't sure whether sustainability was going to end up on the sidelines of finance or whether it would become fully integrated, but I have always been a business builder and I welcomed the opportunity of an ill-defined challenge and of creating something. I would like to think that I understood its full potential, but I could not have conceived then that sustainability would pervade everything we do in banking and in the broader financial services arena. Timing and a bit of luck is everything, as they say, but one does have to be open when the chance to take a considered risk is put in front of you.

Emerging markets

Fast-forward to today, and I am the Chief Sustainability Officer (CSO) of Standard Chartered, a special, mission-driven organization with a brand promise to be "here for good" underpinned by a genuine commitment to sustainability. I work with a tremendous team that is full of energy and ambition and who recognize that in emerging markets, where we have a significant footprint, much of the sustainability story is yet to be written.

What we do know is that emerging markets are often most exposed to the risk from the impacts of climate change and social inequalities. Much of the work done to date has been geared toward the needs and expectations of the global West, but if we don't consider emerging markets as part of the solution, we will not achieve the needed progress in transitioning to net zero. The meaningful participation of markets such as India, China, and Indonesia is crucial. For instance, accelerating the decommissioning of coal and finding a way to move quickly without leaving hundreds of thousands of people with no access to jobs or energy is a serious environmental, social, and political problem.

To solve thorny issues such as these, I am focusing on the bookends of sustainable finance: fostering true innovation at the speculative end on the one hand, and scaling much more of what has worked well to date, such as raising capital in the public bond markets for sustainable and green finance, sustainability-linked instruments, and project-financed clean energy programs, on the other.

Meanwhile, we are also working hard on mobilizing capital for adaptation, which isn't currently well understood or well defined by the markets. Today, there aren't many instances of private finance going toward adaptation projects, particularly those focused on natural capital solutions, but we aim to change that. Opportunities that look at new models for resilient agriculture, sustainably managed reforestation, or mangrove restoration in coastal regions can all play a part. And importantly, alongside having a role in addressing climate change, nature-based solutions can promote improvements in biodiversity. As our 2022 report *The Adaptation Economy* indicated, we need hundreds of billions of dollars to be invested, and the longer we wait, the worse it gets and the more it will cost.

An ever-changing role

Getting investment to where it is really needed neatly explains the changing role of the CSO and highlights the changing attitudes in the financial services sector toward sustainability. In the mid 2010s, people coming into the CSO post, or an equivalent role, would have been more likely to be adept in telling the story of the positive things the organization was doing, rather than necessarily having a strong banking background. Alternatively, the role might have seen someone coming from the risk side of the organization, with many banks engaging in sustainability from the perspective of mitigating the risk of physical or balance sheet asset losses from climate change.

Currently, if the role isn't linked to the commercial or revenue-generating side of the business, I believe the organization is missing a trick. I am seeing origination bankers, structures, and capital markets experts coming from the business side and very effectively bringing sustainability and the bottom line together. The primary reason banks will remain in business is because they are serving their clients and because they are producing profits for shareholders, both of whom give us the license to operate. Of course, we have many other very important stakeholders – regulators, civil society, the planet, and our employees – but if we aren't making a profit we will ultimately be out of business. Therefore, we should not position sustainability and profit motivation as mutually exclusive. That is what practitioners in sustainability continuously need to demonstrate. Proving the notion of profit-enhancing purpose, and the reverse, has really helped me, and the teams I have worked with, create some breakthroughs in the sustainable finance space.

One of my proudest achievements in this most recent phase of my career was creating a series of private vehicle instruments for commercial investors looking to help preserve the oceans while generating market returns. It wasn't previously a focus area for private finance, or not at scale, at least. Many smaller investments had, at the time, raised money – usually through venture or philanthropy capital – but we were able to prove you can get mainstream investors to deploy hundreds of millions of dollars to protect oceans. People also said you couldn't invest in animal conservation and make returns, but we were able to create a blended finance vehicle geared toward saving endangered rhinos. That was a big breakthrough.

Former teammates and I involved in these transactions still talk about them with pride and enthusiasm. They were meaningful and gave people hope and excitement. These examples showed others what could be done and led to similar products coming to market. Imitation is the sincerest form of flattery, but, more importantly, it leads to more capital being deployed to help tackle our most profound global challenges.

Intestinal fortitude

However, creating impactful sustainability financial products is just one part of a CSO's ideal competencies in a bank. Being resilient and having a thick skin are equally important. With the CSO role being relatively new, someone in the role may often find themselves trying to convince colleagues of sustainability's place in the mainstream business. Some won't immediately see your vision for sustainability embedding, others will be skeptical about its commercial viability, and still others may be worried about the impact on their clients of pursuing the agenda too quickly. At the end of the day, however, the job is one of being a 'change agent,' and therefore you must have intestinal fortitude!

You also must be nimble and able to deal with the uncertainty associated with a dynamically evolving operating environment. In this space, what was 'green' yesterday might not be so tomorrow; regulations and standards are rapidly changing and you're constantly trying to help yourself and your clients to keep pace with the change.

I'm often asked what advice I would give to someone looking to get into the field, and it starts with finding a role that attracts you. As sustainability is now a factor in every role, if you build the foundational skills in the given field – relationship banking, capital markets structuring, law, compliance, marketing, communication – and then determine how sustainability features in that field and adds value, that's the best way to find your entry point.

I am also asked about the high number of women (and particularly very senior women) in the field. Conventional views suggest it is because women, more than men, are primary caregivers and care more about the legacy they're leaving to their children. While this no doubt is a factor, I'm not sure it entirely explains the dynamic. Men also care deeply about the future of the planet and are equally passionate about making an impact.

I have been very active for a long time in championing women in financial services, but the numbers have been slow to move in traditional senior positions (although this is changing, and I am thrilled to see my firm ranking among the very best for women in senior executive roles). I think one of the reasons women have made such great progress in sustainability is that it is a less mature discipline. In sustainability, we don't have the legacy issues some positions have; there isn't a long history of male leaders promoting in their own likeness. In this field, there are few role models, so you can parachute a talented woman into a CSO role and they are able to mold it to their own likeness and vision.

An evolving sector

While the role of the CSO is evolving, so is the sustainability sector. As we look to the future, there are several urgent things we need to focus on as we pursue a just transition to net zero. One is common definitions. We want to scale transition finance, for example, but we don't have a widely used definition of 'transition.' Right now, the sector is increasingly reluctant to use 'transition' as a financial product label due to greenwashing concerns, which is causing the public capital markets for products such as transition bonds to stall.

We also need policy support and collaboration to create the enabling conditions that facilitate financing flows, whether it is capital treatment, labeling legislation, or harmonization of sustainability disclosure standards. When regulators in different markets are producing different or conflicting regulations governing sustainable finance, how can global practitioners operate efficiently and how do global investors understand best practice?

Apart from globally implemented advances in sustainable finance practice and governance, the acceleration of innovation is critical. Many of the technologies that will help us transition to net zero are yet to be created. Meanwhile, some of the tech that does exist is at an early stage and will need to evolve significantly into the final use case before it can scale at global levels.

A good example is electric vehicles (EVs). EVs have been our great hope in weaning the personal transportation sector off petrol but the first generation of cars haven't been accessible for the masses. The cars were too expensive and the battery life limited penetration. Even as of 2023, the biggest barrier to entry for EVs is the lack of adequate charging infrastructure. Battery charge anxiety has become one of the biggest barriers to sales. Needed innovation falls into the camp of that which is revolutionary – such as EVs as a concept – but also that which is evolutionary, for example, extending the range of batteries and investing in the infrastructure to support wider adoption.

Ultimately every industry, not only those well known for producing the highest carbon emissions such as fossil fuels and transportation, will need innovation in some form to reach net zero. In the food sector, we need technological and business model disruption in how we grow, preserve, and package our foods. In the fashion industry, we need advances in textiles that can help us supply the input chain with more sustainability. This sector has a significant impact when you consider the resources involved and the prevalence of fast fashion encouraging ever greater consumption.

Culture change

Yet it's not the only thing we need. We need people behaving in a less consumptive and more responsible way, from small actions such as turning the lights off when we leave the room to personal purchasing choices – the more we buy, the more we waste, and what we buy matters because the power of the wallet drives a response from suppliers. Consumers are demonstrating an appetite for change even at a marginally higher cost, so the potential here is tremendous.

Perhaps the most important recent issue to tackle is to depoliticize sustainability. How can saving the planet, and thereby our very existence, be political? It feels like something we shouldn't be arguing over. There needs to be a global recognition that if we don't act, and act quickly, we will only have ourselves to blame.

Looking to the future has made me consider my past, and the question my chief executive asked me all those years ago is still at the back of my mind, informing what I do. As for my own legacy, perhaps the most exciting part of working in this field is that I am constantly challenged to do things that many think are too hard or can't be done. This is an important motivator for me. Down the line, I really would love to think that I was able to make an enduring impact in our most important sustainability challenges and that I inspired others to do the same. The legacy question asked and answered!

29   The world we eat

Marta Antonelli[*]

As a child, I spent a lot of time at my great-grandparents' house in a small village on the outskirts of Rome. Built by my great-grandfather in the aftermath of World War II, it was set within great, beautiful folds of countryside – and seemed always wrapped in beautiful sights and scents. These were things I couldn't get in the city where I was born and raised (even if Rome is the greenest and largest agricultural municipality in Europe).

My great-grandmother was a farmer. Her hands were hardened by a life spent working in the fields, her skin darkened by the sun. I remember how she would return from the garden: fatigued, smelling of earth and soil. But she was always beaming with satisfaction, showing us the fruits of her labor – vegetables, strawberries, grapes, nuts. Their flavors are printed in my memory. I still find myself searching for them.

My passion for nature and food dates to these sweet memories. During those walks in the countryside, and frequent visits to my great-grandmother's vegetable garden, I began to think about what was *behind* the food we ate – and the essential role that nature played. Above all, I was captivated by her connection to nature as somebody who 'worked' the land, by the labor that goes into *producing* food. I saw that it was all about managing scarce resources – soil and water – to create the perfect conditions for growth.

It's not just about food

Much later, studying for my PhD at King's College London, my supervisor – the Stockholm Water Prize Professor Tony Allan – would remind me of the following: "Farmers are the world's most important natural resource stewards and managers. We need them to transform the food system. We

---

[*] Head of Research Barilla Foundation & Advisor

need to provide them with the means to be sustainable. They deserve to be fairly compensated for the ecosystem services they provide."

I learned that it wasn't *just* about food – that within agriculture are embedded a vast range of resources and values that are invisible to the naked eye.

During my very first course at university, I was transported back to my great-grandmother's garden: "If you want to change the world, start with agriculture – we all depend on the millions of farmers around the world who produce food and ensure our food security globally." This was the mantra of the professor who taught Agriculture and Development – an introductory course that opened my eyes to the shape of this 'invisible' world. Her research, which focused on the plight of women farmers in India, was pivotal, and her words stuck with me throughout my years at university. Ultimately, they helped me to think about how I would make my *own* contribution to changing the world.

Water

This all became clearer a few years later, when I discovered a book that would change the course of my life: *The Water Wars*, by Vandana Shiva. Turning the final page, I knew I wanted to find a way to reconcile our eagerness to grow and accumulate with the necessity to preserve and respect.

Later, in 2009, I started working in the sustainability field as a researcher, eventually becoming a consultant for the for-profit and non-profit sectors. And water was the perfect place to start.

Having wrestled with complex theories around human and physical geography, political science, and development economics during my PhD studies, I jumped head first into the concept of *virtual* water. Virtual water is the water that has been used to produce food products in all phases of the supply chain. Most of it refers to water used in farming to sustain crop growth – a truly enormous volume of it. Between precipitation and irrigation, over 6000 liters of water are used simply to produce the food that a single Italian will consume, on average, over a single day. The concept explains what is truly embedded in the food production system – giving shape to the 'invisible' world that's hidden behind the products we see on supermarket shelves.

Unraveling the importance of water in food production, consumption, and agricultural trade became the focus of my professional activity as a researcher until the mid-2010s, leading me to publish a book – *The Water We Eat* (2013) – that first brought the topic to Italian audiences. This publication was the first of many others that, starting from our *footprint* on water resources, extended, more broadly, to the sustainability of food systems, moving beyond the purely environmental to consider social and economic dimensions.

Until the mid 2010s, sustainability was a concept that only a select few spoke about – scientists, activists, NGOs, and a handful of inspired business managers. Today, everything has changed. There is a new awareness, from the political to the business level, that sustainability must be embraced – not as a *nice to have* but as an *imperative* to survive in a world increasingly constrained by climate change, biodiversity loss, and ecosystem degradation, all of which exacerbate inequalities, trigger conflicts, and cause major disruption.

Today, it is widely acknowledged that paying attention to ESG issues is critical for all companies across all industries. It is also claimed that ESG programs will generate more shareholder value in the future, vs. what they do today.

Choose change

But big statements and good intentions are no longer enough. Change needs to happen at the level of the individual – as citizens, consumers, and eaters. Helping people and organizations embark on a more sustainable journey – and create value from this purpose-driven transition in the food system – is my mission.

A big portion of my work is devoted to promoting healthier and more sustainable food choices, to mitigate climate change and water scarcity. Although it is often downplayed, the food system accounts for up to 37% of anthropogenic GHG emissions and is the biggest water user globally. Scientific evidence shows that the adoption of healthy diets can reduce the number of premature deaths considerably (where poor diets are the biggest modifiable factor risk of several diseases) while also remaining within the safe operating space of the planet.

Cooks, chefs, and consumers are key targets of the projects and interventions I have contributed to designing and carrying out, with vital support and funding from the European Union, which has committed, with its Green Deal, to achieve climate neutrality by the year 2050.

Let me illustrate this approach with Su-Eatable LIFE, a project I steered between 2018 and 2021. Here, I had the chance to engage with workplace and university canteens across Italy and the United Kingdom (including Ducati and City University London). The aim was to help them reduce the environmental impact connected to the meals they served through the proposal of tasty and nutritious sustainable dishes. These emerged from a dialogue with several stakeholders – from caterers to canteen users. The result saw a reduction in both carbon and water footprints. But, to make a real impact, such programs must be scaled up.

Motivating people to eat in a different way is far from easy. Food choices are determined by numerous factors (taste, cooking skills, time, attitudes and knowledge, habits, the price of food) that interact in complex ways. In a nutshell, food choice has an intrinsically personal and irrational dimension that makes it very difficult to engage with in rational ways. Today, my work with European cooks and chefs in the LIFE Climate Smart Chefs (2022–2024) project aims at helping the food sector's operators to combine knowledge on food, climate, and nutrition with their ambition and creativity, to show that we don't need to abandon taste to accelerate the transition. For this purpose, we are designing a high-level training course that is aimed at building climate-smart chefs who, through their work in cafeterias, restaurants, and canteens, can inspire a new culture of eating, as well as a digital tool that will enable them to design new recipes that do not exceed sustainability thresholds.

Life lessons

Throughout my fifteen-year career in the sustainability field, I have learned three key lessons.

The first is that you can't manage what you can't measure. Accounting for the environmental impacts of food means bridging different disciplines (nutrition, health, political science, economics, and psychology, just to name a few). It's essential to hold complex and often uncomfortable conversations that embrace the gray areas instead of sticking to the black and white. We need to recognize that the food system – what we eat, how we eat, and what goes *into* what we eat – is often nuanced, and there is rarely a single solution.

Secondly, to transition our food system we must engage in dialogue with multiple stakeholders, collaborating – over shared goals and interests – to create meaningful solution pathways. This process can be enabled by a more effective use of the knowledge, information, and tools that we have at our disposal. It has been demonstrated that, despite the scientific community having already developed data-driven tools to capture facts and knowledge, these tools are still poorly deployed. We must change this.

The third lesson is that knowledge can be used not only to inform but also to empower. Building a sense of power and accountability in individuals – by designing new campaigns, tools, and other interventions – contains within it the seeds that will change our world for the better. But this journey can only be accompanied collectively, *together*.

30 Giving money a meaning through sustainable investing

*Martha Ra**

Money is often accused of all sorts of evils. But I believe that every individual has the power to give money a meaning of their own, a *positive* meaning. I will share my own story to turn your perception upside down.

My quest began at an early age. I did not attend the local primary school but was sent to a Waldorf school, based on the educational philosophy of Rudolf Steiner. Waldorf schools follow a teaching method that integrates values such as gratitude, responsibility, collaboration, inclusivity, and diversity as integrative aspects throughout the school day. Early on, I learned to value nature, understanding that we should all treat it with gratitude and respect.

From the time I was a teenager, my ultimate dream was to work for the United Nations or an NGO. I wanted to save the world. Becoming a young activist was a natural and logical first step. I joined the World Wildlife Fund and Greenpeace. Occasionally, I even skipped school to attend protests.

How can we bridge investing with doing good?

I went on to study finance and economics, writing a PhD about the risk management of banks. I spent over a decade thinking about different sorts of risk categories, but I never understood why our planet was rarely, if ever, taken into consideration when calculating risks related to investments, especially in the context of private wealth management.

This question always resulted in the same line of thought: Is it conceivable or even possible to combine two worlds that at first glance appear to be completely incompatible – doing good on the one hand and doing well financially on the other? How can this be achieved, assuming it is possible? How can I be involved in reaching this goal?

---

* Co-Founder, Women in Sustainable Finance (WISF)

With my diplomas in economics and finance, combined with the experiences I had gained from working for various leading European and US banks across Europe, I felt a strong inner conflict early in my banking career, that something crucial was missing in my professional life. The career path I had opted for did not provide enough opportunities to do good. The moment I changed jobs and joined Globalance Bank – a Swiss private bank that only invests clients' private wealth sustainably – changed my perception. I realized there were ways to do good with money: by embracing sustainable finance.

What is sustainable finance?

There is no formal definition for sustainable investing. It is an umbrella term for a concept with many different investment strategies. For some investors it means the exclusion of companies or sectors such as gambling, arms, or nuclear power in their investments, based on their personal values or convictions. For others it means integrating ESG criteria, alongside financial metrics, into investment decisions.

Other sustainable investment approaches include thematic investing, where the focus is on opportunities related to one or more specific investment themes, and impact investing. Here, investments focus on companies or projects that generate a positive social or environmental impact. Impact investors typically use one or more of the United Nations' seventeen Sustainable Development Goals (SDGs), including education, gender equality, and climate change, as a basis for their investment decisions.

One factor that these sustainable investment strategies all have in common is that the money they raise is aimed at addressing some of the global issues that the world faces. Even if not all of us are shareholders or investors in the traditional sense, the money that individuals such as you and I invest in sustainable finance contributes to the reaching of these goals. They are small steps toward a better world.

Many investors have realized this, as the rapidly increasing demand for sustainable financial products clearly shows. Sustainable finance has grown exponentially over the past years and the forecasts are equally bright. The size of the global sustainable finance market amounted to $3.2 trillion in 2020, up 80% compared with 2019, as data from the UN's trade and development arm UNCTAD shows. This market is forecast to grow by around 20% annually over the next eight years, to reach $22.5 trillion by 2031, according to Allied Market Research.

Meeting the demand

These figures clearly show that sustainable finance is not just another marketing gimmick or a "nice to have" but is rather an investment strategy that investors demand and that our society needs for the survival of our planet. Yet the demand to invest sustainably is still largely unmet.

My experience in the financial industry has taught me that there are groups or clusters that do not feel represented or actively involved in decision-making. Women are one of these groups. Back in 2018, I was discussing the matter with three friends, asking: How can we put an end to this exclusion? How can we mobilize other women? It was at this precise moment that Women in Sustainable Finance (WISF) was born.

Taeun Kwon, Michele Singer, Edith Aldewereld, and I decided that we could no longer wait to be invited to the decision-making table. We decided to create our own international organization to gather like-minded individuals around us. Working in the financial sector in Switzerland – a conservative and male-dominated industry – was an obstacle to be overcome, but we were no longer willing to accept the status quo. We decided to dedicate ourselves to supporting and accelerating the necessary changes we wanted to see: more women in executive roles and on boards, and the ability to provide women with the tools to make conscious decisions about their private finances and investment decisions.

Even today, too many women continue to rely on their partners when it comes to taking investment decisions. Today, on a global scale, women tend to be less financially literate than men, which represents a further obstacle to achieving gender equality. Half of women in relationships continue to defer financial decisions to their spouse, and – surprisingly – women from the millennial age group (born 1981–1996) do so more than any other age group, as a study carried out by UBS in 2021 shows. More than 80% of the surveyed women responded that they lack knowledge, and a majority pointed out that they have no time to participate in financial discussions because of the burden of their household responsibilities. We are convinced that empowerment is the foundation for taking ownership of our convictions.

The focus of WISF is thus on education: to inspire and empower women to make informed decisions about their private finances, including investments. WISF also lobbies decision-makers, advocates for sustainable investments, and sends representatives to various events as speakers and panelists. The global network today has more than 2300 followers and members, including international companies and family offices.

Even greater impact at radicant

After speaking several times at the World Economic Forum, as well as participating in numerous panel discussions, podcasts, interviews, and educational events, I realized that the means to implement the measures WISF suggests are missing. Sustainable banking and sustainable investments remain the preserve of predominantly wealthy clients.

It was a moment of epiphany when I, for the first time, heard about the radicant bank. The vision of this entirely digital Swiss sustainability bank is to enable a movement for a more sustainable world. Numerous players with similar business models have indeed emerged since 2010, and taken on the outdated business model of traditional banks. However, the investment methodology of radicant is unique. This Zurich-based bank offers financial products that are fully aligned with the United Nations' seventeen SDGs. This matters more than most people realize.

You might think that you already do a fair share for the planet by trying to live as sustainably as possible. You eat less meat, buy second-hand clothes, and source groceries from the local farmer. There's no doubt that this is already a great contribution. Unfortunately, however, private consumption only represents a minor part of our environmental footprint. Knowing how the money that you have deposited at the bank, or any other financial institution, is invested has a far greater and often negative impact than most of us can even imagine.

Our invested money is a major source of CO_2 emissions. An emissions calculator developed by Oxfam France estimates that the amount of CO_2 emissions resulting from a EUR 115,000 deposit at France's largest bank is almost eight times higher than the average annual emissions of a person living in France. This astonishing result is because most traditional banks invest their clients' deposits in unsustainable sectors such as oil and gas.

You are an investor whose choices matter

The money that we invest has a far greater impact on the planet than anticipated. I encourage you to stop for a moment, to sit down and consider how you as an investor would like to contribute to a better world. Which specific causes are particularly important to you? Is it gender equality, education, climate change, access to healthcare – or all of them? When you know how you would like your money to be invested in the future, it is the right moment to act.

A first concrete step is to contact your bank, pension fund, life insurer, or any other financial player and ask them how they invest your money. Sit down with your client advisor and ask about the small print, question the investment strategy of your pension fund, challenge the investments made by your life insurer in unsustainable projects.

This leads to the next concrete step: to start investing sustainably. If it turns out that your money is not invested in line with your principles, replace the financial products that fall short of your ideals. If your bank does *not* offer the desired financial sustainable solutions, then switch banks. Nowadays, it is a surprisingly easy process, where it can take less than twenty minutes to open an account online at a digital bank. There is no need to be a millionaire. At radicant, you can start investing in the specific cause or causes that lie close to your heart with less than EUR 1000. From there, you can track the positive impact of your investments on your smartphone – wherever in the world you are. My vision is that the more people become aware of the actual impact of their invested money, and the more educated they become, the more people will make active choices. This is what I strive to achieve every day through my work at radicant and through my involvement in WISF.

Our investments matter. Sustainable investing gives you the power to influence the future of our society, our planet, and our economy. We can all contribute. Let us bring meaning to money. After all, the power of money is the power of many.

31 Ordinary

Natalie Nicholles[*]

"Everyone, when they are young, knows what their destiny is" (Paulo Coelho, *The Alchemist*). From a young age I was bewildered by the randomness of inequality. I remember standing in my avocado-colored bathroom, looking through a small window onto the garden, and realizing that I was lucky. And it was completely and utterly random. I could have been born in a country riddled by drought, war, or disease. But I wasn't. I was born here, in south London. As this realization emerged, so did a strong sense of purpose: to help people who had not been so fortunate, "because if I were on the other side of the randomness, I'd want them to try to help me," I thought.

Born to a British father and Belgian mother, my upbringing was predominantly working-class south London, with summer holidays spent in the Belgian countryside. My mother had grown up in Africa, where her parents had taught at university in the Congo as part of the transition toward independence. In her early twenties she came to London as an au pair to learn English, with dreams of traveling to Italy afterwards. Once she met my father she settled in London, where she lives to this day.

My father had left school at age fourteen and worked as a TV engineer. We lived in a house with our extended family. My grandparents occupied the ground floor, my aunt, uncle, and cousin had the middle floor, and we had a small flat in the eaves – my parents, brother, and me. For what we lacked in material possessions we made up for in an abundance of love and fun. When I went to university, I was the first on the British side of the family to do so.

The straddling of these different worlds in the eighties and nineties – culture, class, language, race – set the scene for my work to come, affording

---

[*] Senior Director, Capitals Coalition

me a sense of curiosity about other cultures and peoples, and therefore the ability to adapt and learn. It allowed me to work and live in places from Brazil to Bangladesh, France to Niger, Kenya to Australia.

Who am I? An ordinary woman with a clear sense of purpose.

Economics as if people and planet matter

I started studying business in school and was really drawn to the potential for the market to deliver public good; here was a seemingly 'efficient' system that could do so much to shape and support society and the planet. Because businesses were run by people, and people were inherently good, then surely businesses could do great things. Or so I rationalized at age fifteen.

There was little opportunity to push my perspective in the context of the neoclassical economic and management teachings of the 2000s, but I did so at every opportunity. My final-year dissertation at university was on the public's ability to regulate for CSR (conclusion: weak ability), and while on a graduate scheme for a FTSE 100 company after university, I designed a project that sought to deliver social impact through commercial activity (the idea was not taken forward, unsurprisingly).

The graduate scheme was for a company called Wolseley Plc that specialized in selling building and plumbing materials. It was incredible training; it allowed me to work across the United Kingdom and France and manage three £1 million bathroom showrooms in London, as well as gain a forklift truck driving license. My foray into the private sector taught me to learn fast, present to and network with CEOs, motivate a team, and problem-solve, resulting in me turning around struggling businesses. However, this corporate experience was always a means to an end, and I left to set up a project to rehabilitate leprosy sufferers through a change in economic activity in rural Bangladesh. Living and working in a hospital was where I learned the importance of outcomes in decision-making and how international development treats the symptoms of inequality, not the cause.

When I returned to London, I joined NEF (New Economics Foundation), an independent think tank whose vision of the economy *as if people and planet mattered* connected with my vision of the role of business and the economy. I successfully grew its social enterprise, NEF Consulting, working with charities, social enterprises, and governments in the UK and internationally. Here I was both a social impact practitioner, speaker, and trainer, but also a leader and manager of an exceptional team of new economic practitioners who innovated to value wellbeing, environmental impact, and "all that makes life worthwhile," to quote Robert F. Kennedy. I published and worked on topics including women in prison, employment and training programs, and community-based adaptation to climate change. But after five years, I was frustrated at the marginalization of new economic thinking and thought progress would be faster in the mainstream.

The RSA (Royal Society of Arts), a 260-year-old social change organization, was seeking its first Global Director. I had witnessed an appetite for new economic thinking around the world and understood the lack of infrastructure to support such work. The RSA offered the opportunity to support social innovation through a mainstream audience. Over five years I established a network of RSA charities, projects, and global programming for the 30,000+ fellowships from Japan to Thailand, Australia, Mexico, and the United States, bringing investment, focus, and impact. My biggest achievement, however, was changing the mindset and culture of RSA itself, shifting it from having a parochial vision of system change to having a global one.

Then, in 2018, I sought who was really changing the system and was introduced to the Natural Capital Coalition. The Coalition worked with the system – taking business, finance, and government from where they were to operationalize the transition toward a new economy by valuing our economy's relationship with nature and society. It published the Natural Capital Protocol (2016), which is the foundation of many global sustainability developments, as well as the Social and Human Capital Protocol (2018). Soon after I joined, it united with the Social and Human Capital Coalition to form the Capitals Coalition.

Redefining value to transform decision-making

The Capitals Coalition is a global NGO that is, firstly, a global community of people who believe that the value of our natural capital (nature) and social and human capital (society) must be of equal importance to the value of our produced capital. Our 400-strong community fosters collaboration between business, finance, government, standard-setters, accounting bodies, science, and civil society to change how we measure and value the capitals, broaden the conversation, and develop incentives to change behavior.

That's a hard sell for the mainstream economy. Modern decision-making is underpinned by a narrow focus on creating financial value. This is at a huge cost to the other capitals: natural, social, and human capital. In this way we are often not creating value but simply liquidating assets and claiming the proceeds as profits.

And yet, as we navigate an economy increasingly shaped by the impacts of climate change, nature loss, and social disruption, the continued success of businesses will be closely linked to their ability and willingness to effectively manage their impacts and dependencies on nature, people, communities, and broader social structures.

Today, business leaders require an approach that enables them to drastically shift the mindset of their organizations. But they need an approach that is harmonized with their current processes and can be implemented in the short term without radically overturning current business models or global financial markets. Investors need to better understand their opportunities and risk profiles in new and dynamic global markets affected by environmental crises and socioeconomic shocks, and policymakers must support efforts through the cultivation of enabling environments while enacting smart legislation that provides economic, social, and environmental benefits.

Global intergovernmental agreements such as the UN Global Biodiversity Framework, and reporting frameworks and standards such as the European Financial Reporting Advisory Group, the EU Corporate Sustainability Reporting Directive, the International Sustainability Standards Board, and the Taskforce on Nature-related Financial Disclosures, are all driving global momentum for large businesses and financial institutions to assess and disclose their impacts and dependencies on nature (the Coalition is heavily involved in all of them). But we know that we will not be successful at reversing nature loss or mitigating climate impacts without understanding and acting upon these issues which also intersect with social and human considerations and economic realities. This is where sustainability meets economy.

Systems change for business

Through our work we see that the more a business engages in today's interconnected world, the more complex and vulnerable decision-making becomes. The intricacy required to navigate a business through complex value chains, within stressed ecosystems and growing global inequality, while meeting the needs of all stakeholders, is overwhelming.

It is becoming increasingly understood that the economy's persistent emphasis on financial capital as the sole indicator of success across nations and businesses is short-sighted and not enough to carry a business through the century ahead. To evolve the next generation of successful, resilient businesses we need ways of assessing performance, growth, and risk that take account of the real world. This requires considering natural, social, human, and produced capitals simultaneously. This is why we are doing something hard and brave – writing an integrated decision-making framework for business.

To achieve better insights and make risks and opportunities more visible, businesses must seek a broader understanding of their relationships across all capitals. And we must better contextualize the consequences of these relationships for the business itself and for the stakeholders around it. This is what the integrated Capitals Protocol will do – something that seemed so very far away from reality when I worked at NEF all those years ago.

Will I see the changes in the economy in my lifetime? I can't say. What I do know is that market values have infiltrated societal values, steadily moving us from a market economy to a market society, for too long. The economy of the future needs a new theory of value in economics and a new narrative of the values delivered by the economy: one that values our relationships with one another, in the form of solidarity, fairness, and responsibility, and one that values our relationship with the planet. And I will continue to dedicate my time and energy to making this happen, driven by my sense of purpose.

32   Cold smoke

Roberta Bosurgi[*]

The world is not going to fix itself. The people who are trying to fix it usually come to this realization early in life. Many of the people I work with, investors for social and environmental impact and members of my organization, Impact Europe, have a story of the moment they realized it – a beach choked with trash, perhaps a sea slicked with oil. My story begins in Mongolia.

I expected Ulaanbaatar to be cold. The city is considered the world's coldest capital, with January temperatures plunging to -40°C – a windless permafrost that can freeze tears as they roll down your cheek. What I didn't expect was the dome of black smoke hovering above the city. Usually, I think of hot cities when I think about air pollution: a haze of exhaust, the rattle of overworked air conditioners. Thick, black smoke in a clear, cold sky seemed incongruous.

I had traveled to Mongolia as a part of a collective initiative to strengthen health systems, set up by the corporate foundation I was working for at the time. I was aware of some of the health concerns in Mongolia already, but nothing comes close to seeing it first-hand. When winter sets in, much of Ulaanbaatar's population settles down in yurts, and to stay warm they burn a mix of fuels, both haphazard and hazardous. I picked up a bad cough myself in Ulaanbaatar. When I returned home, my doctor told me it would take six months to recover from the three weeks of exposure to the smoke.

As I went back to work, I continued to think about the people I had met in Ulaanbaatar. Cardiovascular diseases are common, and air pollution is one of the causes (besides a diet no longer suited for the sedentary lifestyle of what was once a nomadic population). But if you're sitting in a yurt with your family, trying to stay warm, taking care of your lungs may not be the first thing on your mind.

---

[*] CEO, Impact Europe (formerly EVPA)

In Ulaanbaatar I saw the close intertwining of the social and environmental dimensions of this problem. What could help to reduce the pollution in Ulaanbaatar? Greener fuel – but from what source? Who would pay for it? And how? And what about the cultural cost for people who have made their homes in yurts for thousands of years?

There are no easy answers to these questions. If they were easy to answer, I might not be here writing this today. Difficult questions are inspiring. They are the fuel to my fire (and luckily, at least the metaphor is carbon-neutral).

Looking for change

I can connect my time in Ulaanbaatar with a period of soul-searching in my career. For years I had been steeped in corporate culture in the health sector. This can be rewarding work, especially if you can connect your efforts to a real advance in health and patient access to care, but too often, I couldn't make the connection. I wanted to feel connected to solutions that fix the world, not just aid growth and profit.

There are many ways to drive positive change, and I continued to search for mine.

Volunteering was a part of this. I spent time in Africa with an enterprise that served orphans of the 1980s HIV epidemic, who were suffering from trauma and mental health issues. At the time the organization was seeking to reorient its governance to be more sustainable and long term, and because of my background I found I could help set them up so that they didn't need to worry about funding cycles and could stay focused on creating impact. It was a valuable experience – helping orphans is satisfying, of course – but it also planted a seed about what these kinds of enterprises could be. What if the organizations that served people and the planet could run themselves more like financially sustainable businesses? What if they could scale like start-ups? And what if we could scale this whole idea and create an economy where making the world a better place is not a fringe benefit, but the whole point?

As I continued to volunteer and explore ways to reconnect with my purpose, these questions stayed with me. So did the reminders, from East Africa to Latin America, that environmental ruin is the daily reality for so many of the world's citizens – people who live in ravaged landscapes, where twenty-year-old cars choke the roads, and who spend their time fearing floods and wildfires. My exposure to the degradation of our planet and its biodiversity started incidentally but became constant. By the time I left the corporate world, I didn't need to search for reminders that the planet needed fixing, and people needed solutions – these reminders were everywhere and occurred daily. And when I looked for answers – What can I do? Where do I start? – my experience led me to the root causes, something most of the people I know in the world of impact investing focus on.

Solving an environmental challenge can rarely happen in isolation; you must consider the people and systems affected as well. And while there may be many causes at the heart of a given social or environmental problem, if you look deep enough, you can usually find a systemic flaw. The flaw I noticed, over and over, was economic in nature: economies designed for growth and enrichment instead of positive outcomes for people and the planet. Extraction instead of regeneration.

Those entities that have done the most damage to ecosystems have operated under the assumption that unlimited growth is possible. It may be possible, but the toll is an unlivable planet. I believe we need to shift this mindset if we really want to have a world that's green and fair for all. Carbon reduction, salvaging biodiversity – these are necessary activities, but they are not the whole picture; changing the way we think about business will also be necessary.

More questions to fuel the fire: How do we build an economy that can effectively put people and the planet first? How do we realign social values to make this work? How do we change the way we do business and live to ensure our planet remains livable?

Looking for answers

There's no shortage of answers to these questions (indeed, I believe you'll find dozens of viable answers throughout this book), but the answers I found, and to which I'm devoted professionally and personally, often take inspiration from philanthropic ideas. This was not something I realized immediately. I had worked for a corporate foundation, and I had first-hand experience volunteering, but I had long held an assumption that the work of philanthropy and the work of business were forever to remain siloed. My current work, as CEO of Impact Europe, breaks down these silos every day. It proves that the good ideas from business – the modern financial and investment toolkit, for instance – are very applicable when it comes to running an enterprise with the goal of making the world a better place, whether that's a social business, a foundation, or anything in between.

As Europe's investing in impact networks and organizations, we put these goals at the core of our culture. I'm fortunate to be surrounded by people who come to work every day with the big ideas of preserving the planet and fixing inequalities. And I'm fortunate that we share this overall goal with our members: accelerate positive change. That's what we do.

As to how we do it, we unite capital providers (impact funds, foundations, corporate social investors, banks, public funders) and social innovators of all sorts. These have an impact on people. They are the heroes making impact happen; my team and I are in the background, making sure they have the resources, connections, research, and peer-learning they need.

An investment for impact is a patient one: it needs time to address the root causes, prioritizing positive change for people and the planet (ideally both!) over financial returns. While mainstream finance often searches for a deal that addresses a gap, our community flips it around. We start by asking the question: What problem are we trying to solve? And then we patiently invest for that. With each of these investments, the aim is the long-term financial sustainability of the enterprise – to give it the ability to keep on cleaning up water systems, or providing jobs to refugees, or solving any other of the infinite challenges today's world presents. If enterprises with social and environmental impact can be allowed to thrive, scale, and prove their successes, then we will be one step closer to the dream of economic systems that are also aligned to these goals.

Our community is willing to put in the capital, the time, and the work to see the systemic solution through to its end. It's inspiring to be around these long-term thinkers, just as it's inspiring to work in a sector where women are often in leadership roles. And speaking of gender, many investors for impact make gender-lens investing a part of their strategy, in some cases when their core goals are for a different theme – again, these are people who see the interconnectedness of social and environmental challenges and strategically connect the dots.

Celebrate the people

I personally celebrate the people in our space, and that can mean providing a platform to discuss their successes. If you look at some of the data about impact investing, you'll see that the European market grew 26% in 2022 (great!), and much of that is driving real positive change that would not have happened otherwise (even better!). Then again, I often consider the successes on a personal level as well. I met the leader of a social enterprise, during our annual conference in 2022. She was seeking to meet people and find a way to accelerate her agenda. She sought me out in the coffee room, pulled me aside, and told me that it had happened: someone in the audience heard her speak, got in touch, and now they are matching funding to continue the work. That work is for African women working in regenerative agriculture. Sustainable food systems are in progress. The plan worked.

Successes such as these keep me going, especially in the face of all the questions that remain unanswered. What's the most effective way to accelerate positive change for people and the planet? That's the big one, and perhaps we will never have a single, final, correct answer. But fortunately, the community I work with has a lot of brilliant answers; more than that, together we have developed the tools, the network, and the wisdom to act. I count myself lucky to be a part of it.

33   Giving back

Rosa Sangiorgio[*]

In the nineties, working in finance was cool. I had seen the movie *Wall Street* with Michael Douglas several times. My dream was to be on that floor, buying and selling stocks. I loved numbers and had plenty of energy, a perfect combo to start studying economics. I soon realized, however, that the trading I had seen in the movies was not common practice anymore – almost all transactions were digitized. I pivoted my studies toward portfolio management. Analyzing companies inside out to build successful portfolios for wealthy clients seemed exciting. I had found my calling! In the next fifteen years I worked in Luxembourg, Rome, and Zurich. I managed portfolios for private and institutional clients, traveled around the world, and overall felt very lucky.

Above all, I was grateful to my family for having given me the opportunity to discover my talent with their full support, to my mentors for their precious advice and the push to always do better, and to all the people I had met who had given me the courage to keep moving forward. The sense of gratitude is often accompanied by the desire to give back, so I started volunteering.

It was 2011, and I was volunteering with an organization called Worldfund in São Paulo. Their mission was to reduce the historically very high drop-out rate of students in the favelas. They offered training for teachers (teaching teachers how to teach better) and provided role models to kids. I was there for a couple of weeks; every day we would visit three different schools and I would share my story of gratitude and hard work, telling kids that if they kept on studying, they could change the world in the direction they would like it to go.

The very last day of my trip, a girl in the last row of the auditorium raised her hand and asked me: "You are telling us that if we study, we can change

---

[*] Impact Investor, Head of Responsible Investing at Pictet Wealth Management

the world the way we would like it to be. So, what are YOU doing to change the world the way you would like the world to be?"

I was speechless. I was there to inspire them, but suddenly my efforts seemed like a drop in the ocean. That was my 'aha' moment.

During my flight back, I could not stop thinking. I was spending a few weeks a year volunteering, but was it enough? Was it enough to inspire others to work for change? And above everything else ... what change? How would I have liked the world to be? The seed of doubt was planted in my mind.

From ESG to positive impact

At the time I was managing portfolios for institutional investors: pension funds, sovereign wealth funds, foundations. Some of them were starting to question their allocations and beginning to look at ESG characteristics. Mainly they were concerned about their potential reputational risk and were starting to exclude the 'bad guys' from their portfolios (i.e., tobacco companies, coal mining, arms manufacturers). Was that the future world I was contributing to build? Excluding the bad guys?

I did a volunteering trip to Uganda. The assignment was to perform a due diligence review of the Kampala branch of Opportunity International and their project on girls' education. Long story short, it was about group loans to families in small communities, to allow girls to stay in the school system (in a world where only boys had access to school).

That due diligence exercise was my first step toward understanding positive impact. I understood that having a positive impact is not antithetical to good returns for investors and that the risk associated with microfinance projects depends on our definition of risk. The implicit guarantee of a community is far stronger than any balance sheet rule could ever be.

When I returned to Zurich, it was clear to me that integrating ESG characteristics was very different from targeting positive impact. Integrating ESG characteristics in companies' evaluation often means monitoring the influence that E, S, and G characteristics have on its financial performance, therefore mitigating the risk of losses and avoiding surprises. Targeting positive impact (or reducing negative impact) means looking at how companies' products and operations impact the environment and society.

I continued to work with institutional investors and their ESG portfolios, and in parallel I started drafting business plans to convince the organization I was working for that positive impact was an investment strategy in which some of our clients would be interested.

Two parts of my soul were converging. Volunteering was my great eye-opener. Investing is not only about optimizing risk and return. It has an impact on the real economy. Through investing we can ensure that we are putting resources into shaping the future we want to see.

The bridge

The financial industry acts as a bridge between people with money and people with ideas. Unfortunately, in recent decades we have built such a powerful financial industry that sometimes we forget that finance is at the service of the real economy. It is as if, on that valuable bridge, we have built a very tall, complex, and profitable tower. As pointed out by a range of economists, innovation empowered by the financial industry has repeatedly revolutionized possibilities for humankind. It was about water power in the 18th century, then the fossil fuels and steam power that made the industrial revolution possible; this was followed by three waves: electrification in the early 20th century, the space age of the 1950s, and the recent digital revolution.

The next wave of innovation is what some environmental economists call "the sustainability revolution," with visionaries and entrepreneurs crafting products and offering services that reduce our negative impact on the planet and progressively aid regeneration.

It's time for the entire financial industry to recognize this change of direction. And we need to build the right instruments to facilitate financing it. Finance finally has the opportunity to become cool again. Will we seize the opportunity?

Growth at all costs

The financial industry we experience today was built on the false premise of infinite growth. Our generation was educated on textbooks from the 1960s based on theories from the 1850s, focusing on GDP as the only measure of progress. Those economic theories expected economic growth to reduce inequality, but it didn't. We are now hoping that economic growth will help us reduce our negative effect on the planet, but it won't.

We accepted the investment thesis of infinite growth, despite knowing that we live on a finite planet. Donella Meadows asked the right questions: "Growth of what, and why, and for whom, and who pays the cost, and how long can it last, and what's the cost to the planet, and how much is enough?"

What if we changed the goal? What if we challenged the idea that we 'need' our economy to grow, whether it makes us thrive or not, and instead build an economy that makes us and our planet thrive, whether it grows or not?

We could build an economy that respects the human rights of every person, within the means of our life-giving planet. This is the essence of the Doughnut Economy envisioned by Kate Raworth: "A social foundation of well-being that no one should fall below, and an ecological ceiling of planetary pressure that we should not go beyond. Between the two lies a safe and just space for all."

What am I doing?

Building such an economy, regenerative by design, requires the work of all of us – citizens, voters, government officials, entrepreneurs, investors. No one will be able to solve everything alone, but together we have a chance. If we look at the existing financial industry, it has powerful resources and competencies that we need to leverage to achieve the objective of wellbeing for all within planetary boundaries.

Buckminster Fuller said: "You never change things by fighting the existing reality. To change something, build a new model that makes the existing model obsolete."

This is my plan: leverage the resources and competence of the financial industry to foster a new model of successful investments that will build an economy that makes us and our planet thrive. I am doing so by leading the Responsible Investing journey of a highly committed wealth manager, and my focus is in creating both awareness and the best practices tools that are needed to meet the challenge.

It's about gathering the right data to assess the investments that we make. It's about advocating for ensuring access to data and awareness by all stakeholders. Thinking about the enormous challenge of keeping global warming below 1.5°C by 2050, for example, it's asking companies to calculate their scope 1, 2 and 3 emissions, and to disclose their commitments. It's about using data to choose which investments to make and providing capital to those visionaries building the solutions to our challenges, or those existing established businesses transitioning toward becoming more sustainable, companies that are scaling renewable energies, or that are sincerely committed to reducing their emissions and have a sound and credible plan. It's about creating awareness by transparently reporting key information to investors, or by collaborating with other financial institutions, governments, and international organizations. It's about taking ownership and supporting sustainable transformation over the long term: engaging with companies and voting at their AGMs to ensure they adopt best practices. It's about fostering long term, instead of short term.

My two cents

We have huge challenges ahead of us if we want future generations to enjoy the richness of life that we are currently enjoying ourselves. We all ought to contribute, as all our resources and talents are needed. Diversity of perspectives is key.

Unfortunately, diversity is as needed as it is difficult to nurture. We all have biases, such as "women are emotional," "white men are unaware," "young people are not trustworthy," or "older people are not able to face current challenges."

What I personally try to do is to manage my own biases. I listen to my thoughts and push back at myself when I hear prejudice in my own language and expression. The differences between individuals are much more meaningful than the differences between "groups," therefore appreciating people for their unique contributions is better than making assumptions about whole categories of people. The best way to avoid biases is both to pay attention to how people are presenting themselves, how they're feeling, and how they're behaving, and to ask questions, tune in, and listen.

When we start listening, it becomes clear that fostering diversity means acknowledging that embracing different ways of interpreting things enriches us and doesn't detract from anyone. In this respect, recognizing and advocating for others is a way to contribute to diversity. I have had to go through my own fair share of "leadership" classes where the objective was to teach me how a "man" would do things. Honestly, I prefer to be myself. As Oscar Wilde allegedly said, "Be yourself, everyone else is already taken."

Sometimes it will be difficult to be yourself, so seek out people whom you admire, ask for advice, find your own squad, and tap into them. Traditionally we have been taught to be competitive with one another because there is a scarcity of jobs at the top. Sorry to bring you the bad news: That strategy doesn't work. The truth is that raising each other up and channeling the power of collaboration is truly how we will change the equation, and we will have a lot more fun along the way. Alone you can have power; collectively we have impact.

34 More than just a product

Rui Yan[*]

I'm Rui, one of the co-founders of PIO. Before we joined forces, Marco, Guanru, and I were three young individuals who shared a passion for protecting the environment. Marco was a serial entrepreneur who worked for Nespresso Innovation, and Guanru was a prestigious product designer in China. We had been close friends for many years and often discussed the environmental issues that were affecting our local community and the planet. During a discussion about the impact plastic-bottled water has on the environment and human health, we decided to create a new bottle that was both eco-friendly and appealing.

Bottled impact

We spent months researching and developing our product, which we named PIO. We wanted PIO to be more than just a bottle; we wanted it to be a symbol of our commitment to the environment and our desire to make a positive impact on the world. Globally, one million plastic bottles are purchased every minute. And these bottles, which take hundreds of years to decompose, end up polluting our oceans and waterways before they break down into smaller microplastics. Studies have shown that these microplastics have been detected in human bloodstreams and in the placenta of unborn babies. We wanted to create a bottle that would address these issues while also being functional and aesthetically pleasing, to make choosing a more environmentally friendly option easier for consumers.

It was designed to be not just a bottle but a statement piece. It was created to be a symbol of a more sustainable future and a reminder that every individual can make a difference. The bottle was made from recycled materials and was designed to be durable, leak-proof, and easy to carry.

---

[*] Co-founder, PIO

After months of hard work, PIO was finally ready for launch. My colleagues and I organized a launch event to highlight our new product to the public. We invited friends, colleagues, environmental activists, and other stakeholders to attend the event and try out the new bottle. The response was overwhelmingly positive. People were impressed with the design and functionality of the bottle, and they enjoyed how the pods gave the water a unique taste.

Besides being the co-founder of PIO, I am also the Managing Director of the Europe–Asia Centre in Brussels, an independent, not-for-profit organization promoting Asia–Europe relations by means of connecting professionals, institutions, organizations, and networks across sectors. Through the implementation of projects, including conferences, workshops, cultural events, publications, and educational and research programs, the Europe–Asia Centre is connecting people and knowledge across continents.

Bottled culture

The success of PIO and my experience working at the Europe–Asia Centre inspired me and my colleagues to expand the product line and create more eco-friendly products. We wanted to use our brand to make a positive impact on the world. I try to combine the two aspects of cultural exchange and environmental protection. Combining the resources and opportunities of the Europe–Asia Centre with PIO's product design further promotes the impact of cultural heritage in product design.

As PIO gained popularity, I realized that we could incorporate our love for cultural heritage into our brand. We were enthusiastic about preserving the traditions and customs of our Chinese ancestors, and we wanted to make sure that our brand reflected that. We began to research the history and found that there were many traditional crafts and materials that could be used in our products. We decided to incorporate these elements into the design of our bottles, giving them a unique and distinct appearance that paid homage to our cultural heritage. The team worked closely with local artisans to create beautiful patterns and designs that were inspired by traditional art forms such as calligraphy, embroidery, and pottery. We used these designs to create a series of limited-edition bottles that were not only eco-friendly but also visually stunning.

The response to the limited-edition bottles was overwhelming, and the team knew that we had hit upon something special. We decided to continue incorporating cultural elements into our designs, making sure that every bottle we produced reflected our cultural heritage. As our brand grew, we began to sponsor local events and festivals that celebrated the traditions and customs of our hometown. We donated a portion of our profits to support cultural preservation projects and worked closely with local communities to raise awareness about the importance of preserving cultural heritage.

The PIO brand became more than just a symbol of eco-friendliness; it became a symbol of pride for our hometown and a celebration of our cultural heritage. We were thrilled to see how our brand had grown and how it had brought people together to celebrate our shared cultural identity. We realized that our brand was not just about creating eco-friendly products, but it was also about preserving our cultural heritage and passing it on to future generations. We hoped that our success would inspire others to do the same and that we could play a small part in keeping our traditions and customs alive.

The PIO brand represents the perfect combination of eco-friendliness and cultural heritage. It is a testament to the power of entrepreneurship and the importance of preserving cultural traditions. Marco, Guanru, and I are proud to have created a brand that not only helps the environment but also celebrates our cultural identity. Our story is an inspiration to all those who want to make a difference in the world and have a positive impact on the environment and our communities.

My colleagues and I will keep dedicating our time to protecting the environment in the past, present, and future. I will also combine my two ambitions with my work to promote the mutual exchange and communication between cultures and environmental protection. I will leverage the platform and all opportunities I have and make my contribution to the world I live in.

35   Be of the mountains

Ruth Oberrauch[*]

I was born in South Tyrol, and the mountains have been a formative part of my identity. They gave me beauty and freedom, and it is here that I continue to live with the family I have built. They are a magical place, a place where I can connect with myself, where I can breathe, where I can recharge my batteries. Mountaineering, climbing, and trekking are a source of constant reflection and inspiration.

When faced with challenges in my work and life, I turn to the mountains. On the slopes and along the trails, the right idea – the correct solution – often presents itself. Here, in the clear air, I can think without distraction, escaping the hustle and bustle of everyday life. They are a place of care and protection.

All in the family

I put these lessons to good use when I went to work in the family business, Oberalp, a group specializing in mountain sports that was founded by my father, Heiner Oberrauch, in 1981. After studying business administration and working abroad for international companies, I returned to 'my' mountains in 2010, joining the family business initially as marketing manager for Italy, for the Salewa and Dynafit brands.

Returning home, I immediately felt the need to develop and bring sustainability to the center of the company culture – an attitude that was already latent in the family via the influence of my grandfather. In 2010, when conversations about sustainability had not yet entered the mainstream, Oberalp was already conscious of these concerns in its attitude, values, and methods. The pieces were there, they just needed to be assembled in a systematic and structured manner.

---

[*] Vice President & Brand Manager LaMunt

Indeed, there was a high sense of responsibility, particularly toward the community. We just needed to organize what was already at our disposal. There was also a history of innovative ideas, such as Salewa's idea of making garments from recycled plastic bottles back in the 1980s.

This was a world that fascinated me, having experienced it during my time in the Pentland Group. As soon as I arrived in Oberalp, I felt the absolute necessity to put everything I had learned into practice: my love for the mountains, for nature, for the environment, but also for people. Since 2011, when I joined, I have dedicated a large part of my time to forming the CSR department within the Group. Today, I am a member of Oberalp's general management and executive board and, in addition to other responsibilities, I am still supervisor of the CSR department. Over the years, we have managed to create an efficient working group that pursues this issue every single day.

In the beginning, this working group comprised the individual product divisions. Together, we worked to build a common language base, defining what was relevant and what we wanted and needed to work on over the next five years. In the process, we constructed a significant working base. Today, this team consists of five people who manage internal and external policies under my supervision. They are a team of experts who constantly liaise with colleagues across every department of the company. For me, it is essential for sustainability to be integrated, for the work to belong not just to these five individuals but to everyone at the company – and in every department. After all, I believe that an objective only becomes real when it is incorporated into every single process within the company.

Within Oberalp, we have an expert for social compliance, and it is their job to oversee sourcing, purchasing, and quality control, ensuring that our standards are met when selecting new suppliers and when monitoring those we already work with. The CSR team expert's role requires them to look closely, to dig deeply. The same principle applies for our Life Cycle Assessment and chemistry experts, both of whom support the development of new products. Behind all this is a rigorous system of reporting and communication. These are essential functions within the company, helping to strengthen sustainability while spreading awareness among our colleagues.

Our yearly CSR report is titled #contribute, reflecting the collective nature of the goals we are setting out to achieve. Ours is a constructive and concrete approach, where sustainability is not a distant, 'theoretical' topic but an issue that touches us every day. We communicate the fact that even the smallest things can make a difference, even if the challenges we face are large and often extremely complex.

Mindset game

In this work, I am convinced that we must not let ourselves be held back by the fear of not being able to overcome these challenges. Sustainability is not and cannot be static; it is constantly evolving and affects all the decisions we are called upon to make. On the first page of our CSR report, we observe the following: "We believe sustainability is not some distant goal, but a mindset, reflected in our daily actions and choices. It's about how each of us chooses to do things. Every day."

We at Oberalp truly believe this mantra, and we put it into practice every day, for long-term processes and those that are more tangible and closer to home. For us, putting things into practice means monitoring and improving the conditions at production sites and finding ways to minimize the impact we have on the environment. Over the next five years we want to lower our emissions in line with the Paris Agreement and, eventually, to achieve climate neutrality. And to achieve this, we are acting on two fronts: first, involving our direct and material suppliers to improve the environmental management of our production sites; and second, by redesigning our future products and reviewing processes with a view to circularity.

This means designing products using low-impact, long-lasting materials that can be repaired and reused. An example of low-impact materials is provided by LaMunt's ReMOCA padding: a lightweight, high-performance padding for outerwear, made by recycling production waste from the POMOCA ski mountaineering skins brand. At the same time, examples of product designs aimed at longevity are provided by the offer of an extensive catalogue of spare parts and repair services from our Dynafit brand, the re-soling services of our Evolv brand, and the 'regluing' for POMOCA skins. Salewa, meanwhile, is working on extending the life cycle of garments with its 'Circular Experience' pilot project at the Bolzano shop, where customers can bring in garments to be repaired, rent mountaineering items, or buy items that have had a 'previous life.'

These ways of tackling climate change are complemented by small initiatives proposed by individuals and brands, for example, my father's idea of the 'Salewa Garden,' which was born at a time when there were many refugees in Bolzano who did not have the possibility of working. As Oberalp, we made a piece of land available at our headquarters in Bolzano and, together with partners, financed and transformed this space into a garden and nursery where immigrants, even today, can grow fruit and vegetables. In this way, in addition to having a job and a small income through sales, they can get in touch with the local community. This is a project that has been going on for five years, to everyone's great satisfaction. And there are many other projects that we support. For example, Dynafit has for years supported the Snow Leopard Trust project to defend and protect the snow leopard – a symbol of the brand – which is at risk of disappearing.

One of the most important projects for Salewa is 'Tirolwool,' using waste sheep's wool in the production of padding, which sits alongside our creation of 'Alpine Hemp,' a natural, durable, and sustainable fiber that can be used in the manufacture of clothing. Alongside these, LaMunt has also developed a funding project to enable girls in mountain villages in Bolivia to go to school, which they would otherwise not be able to do due to the issue of cost. Furthermore, the brand is also very selective and careful in its choice of materials, knowing that the biggest impact lies in the production of the garments themselves. Each brand, therefore, has its own focus, but it is always oriented toward the wider sustainability goals of the group.

LaMunt

It's with this in mind that I would like to tell the story of LaMunt in a little more detail. As the latest addition to the Oberalp Group, it is a new launch that I conceived. The initial idea for the new brand came to me during one of those long mountaineering weekends in the company of my friends with whom I share the same passion. It was from a sprawling chat on the snow, where we discussed how each of us perceives the mountains, that I realized the importance for a woman to express her individuality and her way of experiencing sporting adventure through clothing tailored specifically *for* women.

Today, women's mountain clothing can guarantee high performance, while also allowing us to say something about our female identity. The aim of this new project is precisely to create garments that combine functionality and know-how with aesthetics, thanks to smart fit solutions and sophisticated details. After all, if clothing is one of the expressions of our personality, the challenge is to be able to do so also with technical and functional garments dedicated to mountain lovers like me. More and more women are living the outdoor experience, and they are looking for sportswear designed according to their needs. LaMunt emerges from this realization, embodying a mountain sports brand "created by women for women," and taking a fresh look at the female experience in the mountains. We launched in 2020, during the Covid-19 pandemic. Deriving from Ladin, a language still alive today in the heart of the Dolomites, LaMunt means "of the mountains." It was my grandmother, originally from Alta Badia, who suggested the name: clear and melodic, but also rough and strong, recalling the values I associate with her and all the women of my family. It binds us to our origins.

LaMunt was born under the sign of sustainability, using a wide range of natural and recycled fabrics. It forgoes reaching DWR (durable water repellency) via PFCs (perfluorinated chemicals), favoring sustainability, but without sacrificing performance. When we first started to develop the brand, we defined the basics, the essentials, that every single product must have while setting ourselves clear sustainability goals in their manufacture – including the use of 100% recycled materials. Today, this number stands at 85% – and we are getting ever closer. As a new brand, starting from scratch within the Group, we can afford to apply sustainable choices from the start. And while we have not yet fully 'arrived,' we are well along the way to achieving our goals.

At the same time, the sustainable mindset that guides LaMunt carries across all the brands within Oberalp – and across all our employees. We want as many people as possible to be able to enjoy the wonders the mountains have to offer and for the next generation to be able to benefit from them, too. To make this possible, we have challenges that we can only overcome together. This must remain a shared endeavor, never bowing down before the complexity of the task that confronts us. To protect the mountains, we must be of the mountains. To protect the world, we must be of the world.

36 Financing impact

Sara Bassi[*]

As I sit outside, overlooking the stunning Lake Lugano, I'm filled with gratitude for the opportunity to enjoy this beautiful scenery and ponder how best to convey my beliefs and experiences through the laptop in front of me.

Growing up in different countries from a young age, I had the opportunity to observe cultural diversity and quickly learned to feel at home abroad. Feeling at home abroad goes hand in hand with sustainability, as it means treating every country as my own and cherishing its natural resources, cultural heritage, and communities. In recent years, I have reinforced my belief in the importance of sustainability as a global concept.

For me, sustainability is about discovering our inner selves first, as it is inherent in our nature to care for our surroundings and future generations. In today's fast-paced world, where we are often consumed by various responsibilities and distractions, taking the time to connect with our inner selves and cultivate a sense of mindfulness is essential. With the pervasive influence of social media, it's challenging to break free from the mindset of constant comparison and individualism that is hindering our evolution as individuals. We are evolving rapidly in terms of technology, but the implementation of ESG measures seems to be lagging.

This discrepancy could explain why, despite our technological mastery, issues such as hunger and environmental degradation persist. We're convinced that to escape the 'rat race' and attain financial freedom, and ultimately happiness, we must ignore our emotions and the larger purpose of life. When we are in touch with our inner selves, we are more attuned to the interconnectedness of all beings and the delicate balance of our planet. We recognize that our actions have consequences, and not just for ourselves. Inevitably, this will force us to reassess our priorities and embrace a mindset that goes beyond material wealth and the desire for instant gratification.

---

[*] Financial Professional

People are talking about sustainability as a trend and are not seeing the very visible consequences of overconsumption. We can look back at a historical and widely distributed book, the Bible, observing how societies were provided with guidance on sustainable agriculture in ancient times. Leviticus 25:1–7 instructs farmers to let the land rest during a sabbatical year, allowing it to regenerate and thus promoting long-term sustainability. By not sowing or harvesting crops, the soil is better protected for the future. Similarly, Proverbs 31:8–9 highlights the importance of justice and equity in social and economic systems, promoting speaking up for those who cannot speak for themselves, defending the rights of the poor and needy, and judging fairly. These principles align with social responsibility and fair treatment, both of which are important aspects of sustainability.

Less

From this perspective of social responsibility, I hold the belief that sustainability should not be confined to a specific category or stereotype, and that discrimination and judgment hinder progress and impede the broader adoption of sustainable practices. Just as we shouldn't assume that all companies are greenwashing, we should not discriminate against someone who identifies as a vegan but wears leather. Sustainability is diverse, and we should strive to make it appealing to everyone by recognizing that people have different perspectives, values, and lifestyles. There are ways to integrate these practices into existing lifestyles, whether by reducing plastic waste or conserving energy, or by supporting local farmers or promoting biodiversity. It's a journey, and progress should be celebrated – regardless of the starting point. In terms of governmental regulation, however, I believe that we do need strict measures. Realizing this was a gradual process for me, which is why I place such a strong emphasis on inclusion.

I was living in Milan when the Covid-19 pandemic struck. At the time, I was juggling a hectic schedule with studying, social events, sports, and running a side business. It caught me completely off guard, and I found myself struggling to adapt to the unforeseen challenges it presented. I planned to visit my father for a week and, against my usual tendency to overpack, I heeded the advice to take the bare minimum with me. After several weeks, I accepted the harsh reality that the black swan event had occurred, borders had been closed, and I couldn't return to Milan where my flat and belongings were. For a while, I had to make do with what I had, since I'd never been a fan of online shopping. It was through this experience that I learned that having less actually makes you feel more liberated. In recent years, this has led me to invest in fewer and better-quality garments, slowly reducing my fast fashion consumption.

Taking advantage of market demand, I formed a partnership with a Korean supplier and a Swiss asset manager to become involved in the PPE (personal protection equipment) industry. As a result of many discussions and meetings regarding the huge quantities of PPE that were needed, I learned about the detrimental effects that masks and other PPE have on our environment. In addition to these experiences – and moving to Switzerland, where recycling is mandatory – I gradually became more aware of sustainability and started my journey of bringing about change.

Action

It was while I was spending most of my time at my father's office, due to pandemic restrictions, that I came across a brochure on pyrolysis oil. At first glance, it appeared to be a technical manual only understandable to engineers. I believe we are constantly surrounded by opportunities, but our mindset can greatly hinder us and often holds us back. Fate had it that the engineer behind the project, Mr. Zivo Miladinovic, walked into the office one day and I grabbed the opportunity to ask him about his project. He exuded an air of humility and pure passion that was palpable and patiently explained it to me using simple terms that helped me grasp the uniqueness of it. I was incredulous that such a ground-breaking technology was not being widely marketed or offered to investors. It therefore ignited my entrepreneurial spirit and propelled me to act.

My involvement in this project led me to conduct extensive research on plastic waste. I then became aware of the severity of the plastics crisis we are currently facing and the alarming information that plastic waste takes over a million years to decompose. Furthermore, I learned about different types of plastics, particularly those that have a detrimental impact on the environment. While PET is a widely known plastic and relatively easy to recycle, the real challenge lies in recycling other plastic types, for example, plastic from the automotive industry.

This is precisely where this sustainable patented technology comes into play. Here, the so-called not recyclable plastic is transformed into pyrolysis oil without the use of chemicals and water, and without leaving any waste residues or gas emissions behind. From the output of pyrolysis oil, new plastic articles can be manufactured. It can even be used as an energy derivative (such as diesel oil or heating oil). Diesel oil, which derives from plastic waste that would not otherwise be recycled, is beneficial to our environment as it resolves a critical issue. Diesel oil derived from *crude oil*, however, is not sustainable and should be avoided.

This represents a prime example of what is known as a 'circular economy,' where plastic waste is re-utilized by reintroducing it into the economy. This made me shift my perspective to see waste as profit, fueling my eagerness to distribute these plants to underdeveloped countries. Over the course of one year, working side by side with an engineer, the patented technology evolved into a bigger project that was presented around the world to investors. I felt like I had stumbled upon a remarkable discovery, and it was my duty to share it with everyone.

During this time, I noticed that the lack of knowledge among investors about innovative patented and sustainable technologies, as well as ESG in general, often leads to skepticism and a preference for conventional projects, such as electric cars and renewable energy. I have come to realize that having cutting-edge technology alone is not enough. Despite the media buzz about governments allocating funds for ESG investing, it's disheartening to see that a significant portion of these funds often ends up being invested in established corporations with long-standing track records. I don't want to make sweeping generalizations, and I understand the intricacies and due diligence involved in VC investments. Nonetheless, I believe there are exceptional and ground-breaking projects that may not be receiving the attention they deserve.

Finance for impact

Even though I am no longer actively involved in the project and have started a career in the financial sector, I am dedicated to contributing to environmental protection in my current role. I am passionate about promoting sustainability through the issuance of green bonds. Regulatory requirements, such as mandatory reporting on ESG metrics and the integration of ESG considerations into investment decisions, are compelling traditional banks to incorporate sustainability into their operations. Additionally, customers and investors are increasingly prioritizing ESG factors in their decision-making, and banks are recognizing the reputational risks of not aligning with sustainable practices.

As a result of a course in wealth management that I'm currently taking, I believe that sustainability and the financial sector are not mutually exclusive, and that we have a critical role to play in promoting responsible investing and driving positive environmental and social outcomes as relationship managers or client advisors. I am looking forward to having the opportunity to contribute to the growing sustainability efforts in the financial industry for years to come.

37   Diary of a traveling Mediterranean woman

Sara Roversi[*]

Have you ever felt the urgency to do something, having such a clear view of the future that you hurried to wrap your hands around it? Have you ever felt the need to go fast or go alone because you don't have the time to explain?

This is the feeling and urgency that moves me every day. At forty years old, with the help of my partner, this sense of urgency fuels me as a serial social entrepreneur, an activist, a philanthropist, an explorer, a start-upper, a restaurateur, and, apparently, "the woman who whispers to the powerful." And I have never stopped being a student of great teachers. Yet people also want me to say that I am a mother and a wife. Would I be a good mother or a good wife? Would I pass the grand jury of what it means to be a woman? Or is this where I don't even stop to explain myself?

I am not setting out, alone, to change the world. I'm not so vain, or naive. I am happy to be alive on this planet, and to bear witness. There is more to it than KPIs (key performance indicators), budgets, and financial sustainability. I prefer to imagine the world I would *like* to live in – what it should be, what it can be. But this trajectory of thinking isn't always comfortable. The right path is rarely the easy one. Much of the work I do begins with imagination – to think about it, and only then to design it, working, always, alongside the beneficiaries of the projects themselves. "If you can dream it, you can do it," said Walt Disney, and I like to dream big. And this is all *regardless of* being a mother.

I say this not out of a newfound feminist spirit, of which we can't get enough – especially since António Guterres, Secretary-General of the United Nations, told us on March 8, 2023, that we are only 300 years away from reaching Goal 5 of the UN's 2030 Agenda – but to deliver to you the next piece of my story. After all, the precooked labels we so often apply to people

---

[*] President, Future Food Institute and Paideia Campus

almost always simplify the real forces that animate them. We are so much more than what people say of us. We can *do* so much more.

Land and mindset

The agribusiness system is emblematic of all of this – its complexity, the need for systemic thinking, holistic approaches, the fact that it is a matter of life and death, the urgency, the emergency that descends from it. Food encapsulates everything I believe in – the need to make it a human right, to do the right thing, to make it accessible, healthy, wholesome, democratic, sustainable.

With the Future Food Institute, I work to create prototype enabling platforms for sustainability in its four dimensions; three of these have been talked about since the 1970s (economics, ecology, society), but there is a fourth that, I believe, is indispensable today: mindset. You might also think of it as consciousness or spirituality. Put another way, this is the human dimension. Change cannot happen without it.

I am asked why I returned to Pollica, a small village of two thousand people in southern Italy, after traveling all over the world, working fast and alone and whispering to the powerful – working with urgency. My answer is simple: because everything makes sense here; it is the perfect gymnasium to train the world with a new 'paideia.' We are caught between a set of hyperconnected crises and an incredibly complex future. These crises are manifold: health, environment, climate, economy, finance, humanitarianism, society, and culture. Paideia lies at the deepest level. It is the combination of narrative plots through which we see everything, for it is the building block of culture that determines our own future and that of others.

From here, our society, which for some is already at the dawn of the fourth industrial revolution – the cognitive revolution, underpinned by a profound change in mindset and an enhancement of human capital – can start to repair the fragmented times in which we live. To do this, we must work from a new mutualism – from gestures of extraordinary generosity; from actions supported by a mindset that is grounded in our common wellbeing.

Paideia, in its highest and most holistic sense, is an "integral human formation" inherited from our classical cultural roots. It embodies an inexhaustible lifelong learning process and engages humans and our environment in a relationship of absolute communion and co-creation. This is the training we have been putting into practice every day for ten years within the vast Future Food ecosystem and in our Living Labs, both abroad and at home, in Italy.

Integral ecology

The most concrete and tangible example in this direction is the Paideia Campus in Pollica, an open-air Living Lab and application of this paideia concept, putting the village, the community, the Mediterranean biodiversity, and the intangible cultural heritage of humanity at the center. This enables us to learn directly and experience in the field what "integral ecology" really means. On paper, it represents a unique model inherited from millennia of history, culture, science, encounters, of which the Mediterranean diet is a leading example.

Today, when the whole world is celebrating the power of education and rallying around the need to "invest in people and prioritize education," I respond in this way: Let us not forget those models of integral ecological regeneration that we have inherited from the past, those principles that govern harmony and that nature offers us daily as the mother-teacher of life.

Already, these things are right beneath our noses. There are organizational and mutualistic models that have always characterized our country. The persistence of the Mediterranean diet and lifestyle reminds us that it is possible to bring together the political, social, individual, environmental, cultural, and economic dimensions. Education can play an important role in helping people to understand the benefits, and how to put this into action. But it requires more than 'learning.' It is grounded in feeling and emotion.

Here I will quote Sonia Massari, PhD, Director of the Future Food Academy:

> Education for integral ecology helps communities discover the roots of their successes and challenges as they strive to meet each learner's needs and the community's goals. By building a deeper understanding through dialogue, identifying practical solutions to adaptation challenges, and redesigning scenarios for equitable and sustainable justice, we educators seek to improve the lives of everyone, not just the students in that community.

The concept of paideia for integral ecological regeneration can, then, become an essential tool to bring the Italian education system back to its roots. After all, these are the pillars of our own culture. They are values that speak to the wider human condition, helping us to reconnect science, history, philosophy, active citizenship, and ecology with our education system. The Mediterranean diet is about quality of life, yes. But it's also about mutualism, of respecting people and places. It is a way of living that can teach us *how* to live, uniting all the Sustainable Development Goals – not as a privilege, but as a common right.

Indeed, holding together the complexities of today's world should be the business not of improvised equilibrists but of wise observers of nature and careful seekers of the balance between mind, body, heart, and emotion.

Roots

During the frenzy of my years as a traveler and explorer, I began to understand the inner dimension of humanity – of people. Reconnecting with nature, and reimagining our relationship *with* nature, is a medicine for the soul, and it all begins with food – that most basic and essential of needs. And this importance has been recognized by UNESCO, which has declared the Mediterranean diet to be worthy of cultural protection.

I used to always look at the big picture, missing the local. After the Covid-19 pandemic, I saw the need to return – to look to our roots. This, really, was a return to the inner dimension, to a form of sustainability that is grounded in ways of life, in emotion. Integral ecology can only emerge from the local. But it can be scaled up to the global level. This is manifest in the work I am doing with Stefano Pisani, Mayor of Pollica, and my team. I am no longer going 'too fast.' And we are no longer alone.

You can find the rest of the information about me online – about the G20, Google Food Lab, governments, and multinational corporations. Here, I decided to tell a different and more intimate story. As Wisława Szymborska writes, I prefer value to price; motivation to honor; content to title; the destination of my shoes rather than my foot size. And we still have a long way to travel together, so let us arm ourselves with courage and a true love of life. Let's look to the future, together.

38 Investing in the future

Silvia Andriotto[*]

From a young age, I felt a deep connection to the environment and a strong desire to make a positive impact on our planet. Growing up, I would turn off the faucet while my father shaved, while in our garden I planted trees – fully aware of the contribution that even small actions could make to our planet. As I grew older, I became more involved in environmental groups and activities, cleaning up beaches and collecting litter around my city.

It was during my studies in environmental science that I became acutely aware of the complex laws and regulations that countries adopt to protect the environment. What surprised me the most was the lack of collaboration between countries, with each one focused solely on regulating its own territory, forgetting that we all share the same planet and that the actions of one country inevitably impact others.

While studying law, I noticed the relentless pursuit of profit at the expense of the environment. This led me to believe that philanthropy, which is derived from the Greek words for 'love for humanity,' is inherently tied to environmental protection, and I have always wanted to be part of this movement. As millennials, we need to feel that our work has a positive impact on the environment and society. Mere profit is no longer enough; we need to be part of something larger and more important than ourselves. This is where impact investing comes in.

As a member of the millennial generation, I hold a deep belief in the significance of sustainable tourism. I make a conscious effort during my travels to ensure that my trips have a positive impact on endangered animals and the environment. My recent trip to South Africa was an unforgettable experience, allowing me to contribute toward the preservation of rhinoceroses rescued from poaching activities. This experience was one of the

[*] Family Office Specialist & LL.M University of California, Berkeley

most fulfilling moments of my life, and I wholeheartedly advocate for more sustainable tourism practices.

Building wealth

New generations of investors are rethinking how their wealth impacts the world. A recent study shows that over one-third of family offices are engaged in sustainable investing, and one-quarter are involved in impact investing. According to the Campden UBS Global Family Office Report, this approach is defined as one that incorporates ESG factors into the investment process.

After graduating with a degree in law, I entered the wealth management industry, focusing specifically on the family office sector. I now work for JTC Group, a firm that recognizes the importance of transitioning to a low-carbon economy. JTC is committed to minimizing negative environmental impacts and incorporating ESG factors into its business proposition.

The reason I enjoy working in the family office sector is due to the intersection between business and impact investing. The purpose of a family office – a wealth management advisory firm that serves high net worth individuals or families – is to manage and preserve a family's wealth across multiple generations, looking after everything from investment management to estate planning.

Meanwhile, impact investing refers to investments made with the intention of generating positive social and environmental impact alongside financial returns. In recent years, family offices have become increasingly interested in impact investing to align their investments with their values, generating returns for future generations. Family offices can engage in impact investing in a variety of ways, such as direct investments in impact-focused companies, investments in impact-focused funds, or through philanthropic investments in non-profit organizations or social enterprises. It can also be a way to engage the next generation of family members in the family's philanthropic and investment activities, helping to foster a sense of purpose and responsibility.

At the same time, impact investing is not without risks and challenges. Measuring impact and ensuring that investments are creating positive social or environmental outcomes can be difficult. Additionally, impact investments may not always generate the same financial returns as traditional investments, which can be a concern for some family offices. Overall, family offices and impact investing are two areas that are increasingly intersecting as more families seek to align their wealth with their values and create positive social or environmental impact. It is a mission that fully aligns with my own beliefs and values.

One Earth, Una Terra

During my career, I have had the opportunity to support UnaTerra Ventures, a EUR 200 million growth VC fund focused on accelerating sustainable scale-ups, which are working on solutions for sustainable and equitable living. The firm was founded by a team of experienced investors and entrepreneurs who are passionate about making a positive impact on the world through their investments. The firm is particularly interested in start-ups that are working on solutions related to climate change, resource efficiency, circular economy, sustainable food and agriculture, and social equality.

UnaTerra Ventures offers more than just funding to its portfolio companies. The firm provides hands-on support and mentorship to help founders scale their businesses and achieve their goals. The firm also has a network of advisors and partners who can provide additional resources and expertise to portfolio companies.

In addition to investing in start-ups, UnaTerra Ventures is also committed to promoting sustainability and social equality more broadly. The firm partners with other organizations to advance these goals and encourages its portfolio companies to adopt sustainable and socially responsible business practices. Their track record of managing multimillion-dollar portfolios and achieving great financial returns is truly remarkable, and it demonstrates their expertise in identifying and scaling up successful companies. It's exciting to see a firm that is focused not only on financial returns but also on supporting sustainable technologies that can have a positive impact on the environment and society. Their approach, of combining active investing and growth operations, shows a commitment to helping the companies they invest in achieve long-term success. As a legal expert and family office professional, I leverage my skills and experience to connect and help raise funds for them, and I am proud to support a firm that shares my passion for environmental conservation and is dedicated to supporting innovative solutions to the pressing challenges facing our planet.

Having an impact

During conversations with other experts at the World Economic Forum and its related summits, I had the opportunity to more closely examine the challenges and opportunities that impact and sustainable investing face. The overall picture that emerged was indeed promising.

Impact investing is a growing field, and studies have shown that impact investments can generate financial returns that are comparable to traditional investments while also creating positive social and environmental impact.

At the same time, it faces the challenge of measuring and verifying the impact of its investments. This requires specialized knowledge and expertise, and there is a need to standardize impact measurement across different types of investments. But it may not always generate the same financial returns as traditional investments, presenting a concern for some investors (Whelan & Fink, 2019).

Meanwhile, sustainable investing provides investors with the opportunity to align their investments with their values, promoting positive social and environmental outcomes in the process. It too can generate financial returns that are comparable to traditional investments (Morningstar, 2021). At the same time, one of the challenges of sustainable investing is ensuring that companies are truly committed to sustainable practices and not simply using sustainable language as a marketing tactic. This can require careful analysis of a company's ESG practices and performance, as well as engagement with companies to encourage improved sustainability practices. Additionally, sustainable investing can sometimes require trade-offs between financial returns and sustainability outcomes, and it can be difficult to balance these competing priorities (Morningstar, 2021).

My passion for the environment has driven me to pursue a career in the family office business directly correlated to impact investing and sustainable finance. As a millennial, I strongly believe that we need to positively impact the environment and society. Mindful of the challenges and opportunities it faces, the family office business has emerged as an exciting way to meet these goals.

39   Social impact in your hands

Simona Sinesi[*]

The word 'sustainability' is etymologically derived from the Latin *sustinere* and the English *sustain*. It also refers to part of a piano, the resonance pedal or 'forte' that creates the magic that holds the sound of a note long after your fingers are lifted from the keys. Perhaps sustainability could be explained as the ability to be able to exploit resources in a harmonious and lasting way over time, just as the resonance pedal does.

In corporate circles, sustainability is often broken down into three dimensions: environmental, social, and governance, or ESG. To achieve sustainable development, the three dimensions must complement each other, and they are underpinned by economic sustainability. Sustainable development is the pole star, a map that clearly shows "where we are and where we need to go." When I speak about sustainable development, I prefer to use the term 'impact' because, in my opinion, it better describes the coexistence of economic sustainability and one, or more than one, of the three dimensions (environmental, social, and institutional).

The seventeen Sustainable Development Goals (SDGs) outlined in the United Nations' 2030 Agenda are the operational tools of impact we can use to design a better world, one in harmony with nature and the finite resources at our disposal.

Social

It is the social dimension of sustainability that fascinates me the most, the 'S.' I would say that my parents were right when they gave me a name beginning with the letter S.

---

[*] Social Entrepreneur, Founder & VP of NEVER GIVE UP, University Professor, Author

My career began in 1999, when I joined teams working on global communication and marketing strategies in the world's largest FMCG (fast-moving consumer goods) multinationals, such as Unilever, Coca-Cola, Barilla, and Sony. My experience in social impact began a few years later, in 2014. The triggering event was a trip to Washington, D.C., to see my sister, Stefania, who works there as a psychotherapist in a children's hospital, working on the prevention and treatment of eating disorders. Her work involves supporting parents and their children, as early as the breastfeeding and weaning phases of their development, to foster practices that avoid the onset of disordered eating in childhood.

When I returned, I decided to read up on the subject and learned that nutrition and eating disorders are the primary cause of death from illness among twelve- to twenty-five-year-olds in Italy, and that only 10% of them were able to seek help.

I discovered it took teenagers an average of three years from the onset of their first symptoms to seek help. And finding treatment centers that would take in children under the age of fourteen was rare. The few facilities that did exist were former psychiatric hospitals, and these environments were certainly not suitable for treating children and adolescents.

It was at that time that I felt an urgency to "do my part" and decided to create NEVER GIVE UP, a non-profit organization whose mission is to change the narrative on eating disorders. Our aim is to intercept discomfort with food, weight, and body image early on to prevent disordered eating, and to provide support to young people who suffer with it.

Through my experience with NEVER GIVE UP and as a mentor and advisor to social impact start-ups, I have come to realize that social entrepreneurs are the kinds of leaders we need. Working with an outcome-focused approach, they "shuffle the cards" and identify patterns between people and behaviors that lead to real, systemic change.

Unfortunately, Italy is behind the pack as far as social entrepreneurship is concerned. In Spain, social entrepreneurs have a seat at the table with companies and institutions and other actors in the system that sway societal change.

Marked as a huge win for social enterprise, Spain's Vice-President and Minister of Labour and Social Economy, Yolanda Diaz, presented the first resolution in the history of the UN on the social and solidarity economy ("Promoting the Social and Solidarity Economy for Sustainable Development") to the UN General Assembly in April 2023. "The social economy is our today and our tomorrow": this is how Diaz began to present the resolution at the UN Assembly, marking a decisive historical moment for the global recognition of the social economy and the role of businesses, cooperatives, and other social impact organizations.

This resolution encourages the 193 member states and financial institutions to promote and support the work of social enterprises in achieving sustainable development and invites financial institutions, including banks, to support the social and solidarity economy through both existing and new financial instruments and mechanisms.

At the Glass Palace, the approval was almost as lightning-fast as the approvals for the initiatives of four other major institutions undertaken in less than two years. Other initiatives on social entrepreneurship were also taken up by the European Commission, the International Labour Organization, and the OECD.

New leaders

The complex times we're living through, in which the balances of power and influence are shifting with unpredictable speed, highlights the need to resort to a new leadership model that takes notes from social enterprise and combines business with impact. But no one can solve social problems alone, and there can be no social impact without a systemic approach.

The social entrepreneur acts as the 'facilitator and catalyst' of change. They must not only find new perspectives with which to frame the social problem they intend to solve, but also understand the system to identify the forces and interdependencies of change and the individuals, groups of people, organizations, and institutions that are either interested in solving the problem or maintaining the status quo.

Once the issue has been picked apart, the social entrepreneur needs to be able to change the problem's narrative by finding a new perspective for its resolution. Communication and advocacy are key to being able to generate and maintain impact.

A part of this role is to raise awareness of the societal problem you aim to tackle by engaging institutions, inciting public opinion, and drumming up media attention.

I am always inspired by the story of Professor Muhammad Yunus, Nobel Peace Prize winner, who took a 'bottom-up' approach and worked with small villages in Bangladesh to completely overturn the credit paradigm. It was impossible for people to obtain a bank loan if they couldn't provide the necessary paperwork or guarantee they could repay the debt. This denied many Indian entrepreneurs access to finance and forced many to access loans, on capricious terms, from wealthy merchants or usurers.

Yunus didn't waste his time convincing banks to grant loans without collateral. Choosing to focus on supporting women's involvement in the development of micro-entrepreneurship, he decided to personally apply to a local bank for a loan of 10,000 taka, or \$300, and lend limited sums of money (\$27) to small groups of women, without requiring any collateral.

In 1983, he founded Grameen Bank, which turned out to be a bank with a 99% debt repayment rate. This ushered in a new form of financing: microcredit banking, which has been adopted by credit institutions around the world. When I first met Yunus at the Festival of Economics in Trento, I took from our conversation a message whose most salient passages I quote here:

> Social impact is in your hands, not in someone else's. We are facing an unprecedented opportunity, a historic chance to make the paradigm shift that humanity so desperately needs to bring about a new civilization. We need it because science demands it, because our consciences tell us that we cannot go on like this. Now, more than ever, we need start-ups operating in the field of social business to solve the social and environmental problems that plague the planet. If I were an experienced banker, for example, I would not have created microcredit. All we need is a strong will to solve an existing social problem, without worrying about having to start big right away. We must remember that what is needed to embark on the social business journey is not deep experience, but deep involvement. Experience can lead us astray.

Today, I have the honor of collaborating with Grameen Lab, one of the social enterprises founded by Yunus on the Young Challengers Programme, where I mentor young change-makers who intend to develop a social enterprise. The message I want to share with the young change-makers and with you is that social impact is in your hands, which, besides being the title of my book, is a mantra for all of us as we make sure our future will be better.

40   When we save the planet, we save ourselves

Susanne von der Becke[*]

When the initiators of this book asked, "why do you care about the environment so much?" I paused. Sometimes caring hurts and sometimes it feels like it would be easier to give up. But we care for what we love, and when we see it get hurt, we must act.

The world might seem to be divided between people who care and people who don't. This is a pessimistic view. Studies have shown that our brains are primed for love, and although human history is undoubtedly filled with many atrocities, it is also a history of kindness. We have all seen the newsreels of environmental destruction: of sea birds slowly choking on the plastic in their stomachs, starving polar bears on a desperate hunt for food, and droves of people forced out of their homes by floods and wildfires. Our hearts know that we are part of nature, that nature is part of us, and that we are interconnected, but we're not always ready to process the feelings these images trigger.

Watching the predictions of climate scientists become a reality for people around the world can leave us feeling numb and overwhelmed. We're not only confronted with joint environmental and social crises, but we also face a personal crisis of being. Although historically, on average, people have never been as wealthy, safe, educated, and liberated as we are now, many of us suffer from chronic stress, burnout, anxiety, addictions, depression, and loneliness. The way we work and live is no longer sustainable.

We lost ourselves

Somewhere along the way, we lost our connection to ourselves, each other, and nature. Part of this problem stems from the growth-focused, fast-spin-

---

[*] Founder of VDB Insights & Chair of The Klosters Forum

ning economic system we've built. It is a system that has made some people very rich, but it's based on the belief that self-serving individualism and competition will lead to the expansion of overall social welfare. This approach ignores the complexity of economics, and human nature.

We need a new story. If we want to help solve the environmental and social issues we're facing, we must see ourselves as part of a bigger living system. When we talk about saving our planet, we're really talking about saving ourselves. Doing this requires us to let new ways of thinking emerge, both in our companies, communities, and governments and also as individuals through our inner work.

I have been interested in inner work, healing, and meditation for over twenty years, but I separated it from my professional life. I felt I had to choose between two opposing sides in me: one seeking inner peace and the other focused on solving global problems and action. I considered practices such as mindfulness and meditation a personal matter and did not see how relevant they could, and would, be for my leadership.

Our passions are often strongest when we are young, and once we join the world of work, performance, and competition, we forget about them. I cared a lot about the environment and social justice issues as a child. My father was a journalist, so I grew up with the news and hearing the doom and gloom of the times. I felt a strong sense of responsibility to do something about it, and at some point, I declared my intention to make the world a better place. I had no idea how, and my outburst was met with grumbles of "who does she think she is, does she think she's something special?" from the adults in the room.

I didn't think I was special, and I felt an uncomfortable sense of shame about wanting to do good. And I still see this type of response happening to executives who describe the reactions they get when they first challenge the status quo and want to implement more environmentally or people-friendly policies. It takes courage to do things differently.

Crisis and action

As a student of management at the London School of Economics, I wrote my master's thesis on CSR. At the time, CSR was not part of my curriculum, and such policies were not mainstream. If companies had CSR policies, they were driven by risk, not interest or concern. CSR was not a sexy topic, at least in my circles.

Making money was sexy. It was also an entirely practical objective if you wanted to be financially independent. Working in structured finance, selling asset-backed securities at Lehman Brothers, put me right in the eye of the storm, which would later trigger the Global Financial Crisis of 2008. When I left Lehman Brothers it was due to neither a sudden burst of wisdom nor a premonition of its future collapse. Instead, it was the decision to follow my heart and move to Switzerland, where I now live with my husband and children. When Lehman Brothers declared bankruptcy on September 15, 2008, I was working for a fund of hedge funds and private equity. What followed was an unraveling of the entire financial system and the biggest economic downturn since the Great Depression. And, although I was just a small fish in the pond, I couldn't help feeling responsible for the crisis.

I wanted to understand how the failure of a relatively small investment bank could trigger a market meltdown of such scale, and I embarked on pursuing a PhD at ETH Zurich, writing about financial crises, money creation, and market crashes. It was during this time that I was first introduced to complex systems thinking, which resonated not just on an analytical but also on a much deeper level. The interconnected and fractal nature of our systems, which is directly observable from the outside, corresponds with my inner observations during meditation.

Complex systems are more than the sum of their parts and develop emerging properties through the interaction of their parts. Looking at our current environmental and social crises from a complex systems perspective reveals that everything is interconnected, that change is nonlinear, and that our social and economic systems result from our collective behavior. This helped me to understand that, as individuals, we can feel powerless and perceive the system as something outside our reach while, at the same time, we are contributing to its emergence through our interaction. Take the climate crisis as an example: We are not directly responsible for the whole crisis, but we know that every day our activity is making the situation better or worse.

I already had a regular meditation practice while I was pursuing my PhD. When my mind was full and I was stuck in my analysis, when I was getting frustrated and had no idea where my research would take me, I would sit. I would gather all the data and then sit with it, be with the confusion, not trying to solve it, and let myself become empty – not empty in the sense of having no thoughts, which is impossible, but empty in the sense of having no judgment and no preconceptions. And in this way, without my doing, a new perspective would usually emerge that would lead me to my next step. Being able to hold contradictory views, to be with uncomfortable feelings, to know our patterns and cultivate an open mind and heart are core leadership skills in this increasingly fast-changing, complex, and uncertain world.

Love

Today, I no longer feel like I need to choose between inner peace and outer action. My own inner journey led me to realize that I can experience a sense of peace while I am in action driven by a sense of service. We can create an inner spaciousness that allows us to sit with these dualisms: to see nature's beauty and its destruction, our human capacity for compassion and for violence. I also noticed that the gap between inner and outer, personal time and work, stillness and action starts fading the more connected I feel inside.

My current work as a founder of VDB Insights and chairwoman of The Klosters Forum emerged from my early, but then neglected, passion for sustainability and my continuous exploration of my own mind to overcome inner obstacles that kept me from acting from a place of love rather than fear. I founded VDB Insights to help business leaders and change-makers create positive change for themselves and the planet. Alongside my role as a business owner, board member, and investor, I facilitate inner transformations through mindfulness meditation, transformational breathwork, courses, and retreats. I am also currently writing my first book: a mindfulness guide for business leaders who want to change the world right now.

And when the women who founded The Klosters Forum asked me to join, I leapt at the chance. This non-profit brings together leading thinkers and doers in a unique way. They invite experts from across industries to the Swiss Alps to dive deep into a given environmental issue and create personal connections and collaborations that accelerate positive change. While the conversations are serious, the atmosphere is friendly, hopeful, and fun. History shows that collaboration is our human superpower.

Ultimately, I believe we all care about the future of this planet; we just don't always know how to align our actions with that care. Our current crisis challenges us to act fast but also to pause and reconnect within. I see this as an opportunity to reconnect with what matters and to move from a sense of separation to interbeing, from fear to love. None of us alone will solve our environmental crises, but we can all be part of a new story for the future of this world.

41   Making good money

*Tanja Havemann**

As a child, I dreamed of becoming a veterinarian or a virologist. I had not imagined that I would build a business, let alone a business involved in environmental investment. Now, there's nothing I'd rather be doing. Perhaps it took an unusual background to become one of few female founders in this field; growing up in Tanzania and Kenya and starting out as a scientist turned out to be a helpful start. Over the course of a twenty-year career, I have had the privilege of traveling to many incredible places, meeting many inspiring people along the way. Curiosity, outrage, luck, necessity, and grit have resulted in a career dedicated to green finance.

Studying the environment

It all started in Aberdeen, where I studied Tropical Environmental Science, and in Borneo, where I did fieldwork assessing interactions between soil properties and forest ecology. The contrast between the ever-extending and gigantic geometric monotony of palm oil plantations bordering the seemingly chaotic noisy fullness of the rainforest brought home the dichotomy of nature and "economic growth or progress." I asked myself: Could business not be done in a more equitable and sustainable manner?

This conundrum led to a master's degree in Applied Environmental Economics, followed by a master's degree in Environmental Law and Policy. This new knowledge opened the doors to many more questions, and indeed to some answers. Here, I learned about emerging nature finance mechanisms, such as the UN Framework Convention on Climate Change (UNFCCC) Kyoto Protocol's Clean Development Mechanism (CDM), the precursor to the Voluntary Carbon Markets. In the process, I became hooked on environmental finance.

---

* CEO & Founder, Clarmondial

Serendipity led to me working in a consulting company founded by a former Director General of the Zoological Society of London, Richard Burge, focusing on financing nature-based solutions (NbS) before the term became popular. This experience eventually led me to a role at Climate Change Capital (CCC), a pioneering climate investment firm led by James Cameron, Mark Woodall, and Anthony White, which was both challenging and rewarding. This experience gave me the opportunity to actively participate in financing European renewables, carbon capture, and storage businesses. I later joined CCC's carbon investment team, deploying its EUR 1 billion carbon fund – including in agroforestry and clean energy projects. I left CCC to work on a new 'real assets' forestry and climate fund, then advised other carbon funds, foundations, and NGOs, and ultimately founded my own business in May 2010.

Going solo

Clarmondial was initially founded as a company called Beyond Carbon, working on carbon finance, and affiliated with a CCC colleague, Lizzie Chambers, based in New Zealand. After working on various carbon credit projects, I eventually decided that my interest in green finance was broader than carbon markets and shifted the company's focus to more holistic financing of nature-based solutions and sustainable supply chains, gradually attracting like-minded colleagues to form an impressive team. Clarmondial grew organically in response to market demand. We have demonstrated that it's possible to mobilize additional finance for climate adaptation and mitigation, food security, biodiversity, and ocean stewardship. Clarmondial is now an advisor to leading global organizations and increasingly a proactive developer of new initiatives such as the Food Securities Fund (FSF) and the Biosphere Integrity Fund.

Society is undergoing a paradigm shift when it comes to economics, financial markets, and nature. As we navigate the complexities of this shift, it's critical to stay grounded in the realities of our world. At Clarmondial, we are committed to moving beyond talk and into action, transforming challenges into opportunities for all involved. This approach demands contextual awareness, realistic assessment of all partners' capacities and capabilities, focus, persistence, interest, expertise, and partnerships, helping us to move from ideas to results.

We are also under immense time pressure. The clock is ticking on biodiversity loss and climate change, placing millions of human and animal lives at great risk. Nowhere is this urgency more apparent than in emerging and developing markets and across the agriculture, forestry, and marine sectors.

Our land, our money, our future

Among these, agriculture is one of the most time-sensitive and important sectors. Why? Because the sector is the largest contributor to biodiversity loss, contributes about 22% to global GHG emissions, and employs almost 30% of the global workforce, making it, arguably, the most fundamentally important sector to address if we want to ensure that all humans can live comfortably on earth. This is particularly stark in emerging and developing markets, where global biodiversity hotspots exist, vulnerability to environmental degradation is the highest, and local livelihoods and economies are highly dependent on it. Growing up in East Africa and visiting many rural areas from a young age, with parents working in development assistance, I have seen this for myself, first-hand. But agriculture is seasonal and even large amounts of capital become dramatically less useful if delivered at the wrong time, in the wrong place, and via the wrong instruments. It is difficult to mobilize more investments in these sectors with business-as-usual approaches and intermediaries. That's our role. As we continue to build Clarmondial with our partners, colleagues, and friends, we are continually inspired by the beauty and resilience of nature and people, and we are committed to enabling capital to flow – creating thriving, sustainable ecosystems and societies.

Clarmondial advises organizations that influence global flows of goods and capital, building and implementing new financing solutions in the process. Our clients include Nestlé-Nespresso, Unilever, and the Marine Stewardship Council (notably the Ocean Stewardship Fund). We also support investors to develop and implement strategies that align with emerging regulations and trends, including the EU Taxonomy, Nature based Solutions and climate investments.

A few years ago, Clarmondial took the step to proactively develop new financing initiatives, such as the FSF, in response to discussions with investors and companies. In these discussions, we noticed that there is a lack of scalable nature-related financial products, and a large and growing funding gap for sustainable value chains driven by regulation, investor, and consumer demand. The FSF was developed with an innovative origination and de-risking strategy that harnesses corporates' sustainable sourcing commitments to mobilize additional finance. The open-ended fund, which started operating in March 2021, has quarterly liquidity and creates climate, biodiversity, and livelihood impact through working capital loans. The FSF is classified as an impact (Article 9) fund under the EU's Sustainable Finance Disclosure Regulation. It has attracted investment from the Global Environment Facility, on behalf of the UNFCCC, the UN Convention on

Biodiversity (UNCBD) and land degradation (UNCCD), and increasingly from private institutional investors.

The FSF and our advisory work also inspired the design of a second fund, the Biosphere Integrity Fund – 'Biosphere' – which is being designed with the Rainforest Alliance, Conservation International, and CDP (Carbon Disclosure Project), and is supported by USAID. Biosphere will provide long-term project finance for sustainable value chains that also contribute to positive landscape impacts, including on biodiversity, climate, and livelihoods. We are excited about its investment pipeline and the interest from corporates and investors so far. The FSF and Biosphere Integrity Fund, as well as Clarmondial's advisory work, create a solid basis for continuing to build an independent investment platform focused on nature, biodiversity, and climate. While this will not be easy, it is a privilege to do this interesting and meaningful work alongside a great team.

Opportunities and challenges

The need to redirect capital flows is obvious and urgent. There are many 'guesstimates' of how much nature is worth, and how substantial the financing need is. For example, the World Wide Fund for Nature (WWF) estimates that nature is worth circa $125 trillion per year, and the OECD calculates that the financing gap to achieve the UN Sustainable Development Goals (SDGs) is about $4 trillion per year and growing. The fact is that for human society, nature is priceless. Ironically, that is why we must find ways to internalize it in our economies and financial markets. It's time to redirect resources and capital to nature conservation and restoration. As the leader of a company that consistently designs and implements solutions, I am privileged to be part of the movement that is working toward a better future for both: nature and humanity.

Running a woman-led business is a challenge. Comments are made, such as "how come you know so much," or about my appearance, as well as hints that I am a bad mother because I travel for work. These things are still depressingly frequent, and they must be swiftly, resolutely, and politely dealt with. The time invested asserting credibility and authority could be used more profitably by all involved if that bias would disappear.

Another challenge we face is the emergence of generalist entrants in the nature, climate, and biodiversity investment space, many of whom have little technical expertise and whose structures make it challenging to execute nature-related investment strategies, which often take significant upfront resources and cross-sector expertise. While the volume of investment must grow, poorly conceived strategies implemented without technical and mar-

ket expertise, or a lack of appreciation of local context, will result in negative outcomes and cause a market backlash. This has happened before and
is starting to happen again. This means that there is a growing role for
specialized emerging entrepreneurs and investment intermediaries, such as
Clarmondial. And we are prepared to face these challenges.

42   A fighter

Tessy Antony de Nassau[*]

For each one of us, life holds many surprises. Let me tell you some of the tales of mine. I grew up in Luxembourg, which is geographically extremely small compared with the neighboring countries Germany and France; its land area is about two times the size of Los Angeles, while it is one of the wealthiest countries in the world by GDP per capita, and with one of the most innovative markets globally. From the outside, Luxembourg seems like a charming place with no problems. However, we, too, experience poverty, crime, drug abuse, and corruption. As the daughter of an entrepreneur and politician, I grew up sheltered from most harm while also being exposed to everyday crime.

When I was a child, I learned about nuclear energy and how it can affect our environment and health. The disaster at the Chernobyl nuclear power plant occurred in 1986, before I was even born, yet it is a topic that continues to creep up here and there in the news in Luxembourg. Its impact on the environment and the health of people in Chernobyl and the surrounding regions can still be felt through the spread of diseases such as cancer. Being exposed to such news from a young age made me curious about these topics, which led me to join the military at the age of seventeen, and consequently to write my master's thesis on biological terrorism. I see myself as a person who likes to challenge the status quo, push artificial boundaries, and question policies and laws which do not reflect the fast-changing living and working environment we all operate in today.

Footprints

For this chapter I have chosen one specific time in my life that illustrates how man-made technologies, but also our actions, have an immediate effect

---

[*] Entrepreneur & Investor

on the climate and the environment we live in. As the saying goes, everything you post online will be there forever. I would extend this by adding that all the actions we decide to take will affect our world and the global climate in some way and will leave a footprint; this might not always be seen directly, but indirectly it will be imprinted in the story of humankind. Hence, use this example as a reflection on how actions create environments. As briefly mentioned, I joined the Luxembourg military at the age of seventeen. That would be considered a child soldier by today's standards. It was an interesting time, and I learned a lot about our world. I was deployed as the only female of my draft to the former Yugoslavia, stationed in Mitrovica, with a few hundred men from the Benelux countries as part of the KFOR (Kosovo Force) missions to the regions. My mission was categorized as a UN peacekeeping mission. While deployed, I learned how important it is for a female soldier to be included in the peacekeeping process. I saw my work not only as crucial in terms of representation but also as contributing to solutions to a variety of issues we encountered. In terms of sustainability, which this book focuses on, I have chosen one example from this experience to illustrate how actions can have both positive and negative consequences.

In a military working environment, especially during deployment, there are several factors to consider. One of them is collaboration. The complexity of the operation and its outcome are linked to how people from diverse backgrounds and with diverse skill sets work with one another.

Another factor is equipment. The environment men and women are exposed to and how this environment adds to the skills we develop over time is the story of all soldiers. I remember well the day I was equipped with my kit for deployment. I always carried a dosimeter with me during my five-month deployment. This device measures ionized radiation exposure on the human body. That was the first time I was exposed first-hand to the consequences of how nuclear leakages and chemical waste affect the environment and how this affects the human body. Some of the grass on the grounds around our camp was of an unnatural turquoise color.

NATO reported that over 31,000 rounds containing at least ten tons of depleted uranium were fired in Kosovo. "Depleted uranium (DU) is a by-product created during a uranium enrichment process and is extensively used for uranium ammunition production," leading to an increase in numbers of hematological malignancies, such as leukemia, in most regions of Kosovo between 1995 and 2015.

We often talk about how geopolitics and leadership affect people in war zones. However, the ways in which the ammunition affects the environment and the climate, and its consequences for the flora, fauna, and human beings on the ground, are often underreported. As already mentioned,

I wrote my master's thesis on biological terrorism, and I continue to be shocked at how little these real threats to humanity and the environment are being reported on, exposed, and addressed by global leaders. There is so much to say about this and such little allocation of writing space to it. How all of this is connected is evident to the eye if we are willing to see what is right in front of us. That applies to everything around us, not just the military and the ammunition we use. Wherever we see neglect on one end, there are consequences on another. Everything is connected.

Peace

There are many wars still ongoing, such as the Russia–Ukraine war, Yemen, the Democratic Republic of the Congo, and the Great Lakes region of Africa, and fragile geographical locations and former conflict regions which have unresolved issues that still need to be addressed, such as in the Tigray region of Ethiopia, between Tigray forces and Eritrean troops; in the Sahel, where the governments of Burkina Faso, Mali, and Niger are struggling to contain Islamism insurgencies; in Haiti, where President Jovenel Moïse was murdered in July 2021; in Taiwan, between the United States, China, and Taiwan; and others. We feel and see the effects of bad leadership, shortcuts, and short-term thinking, as well as the lack of reporting, and how these affect people as well as the environment, for example through waves of refugees, instability of markets and economies, the spread of warfare, the use of ammunition and bombs, and the deaths of thousands of innocent people.

Thus, each of us holds a piece to the vast puzzle that is our earth. Our actions have consequences, either directly or indirectly, for the environment. My drive to make this world a better and safer place for all comes from the fact that I am privileged in terms of my standard of living. As such, my approach is not to pursue a philanthropic endeavor or project with a start and end date but rather to get involved in local politics, to stay informed about global crises, and to support projects and people globally in conflict zones where possible. The responsibility lies with all of us, and our actions will determine what legacy we leave to future generations.

43   Shaping another tomorrow

*Vanessa Barboni Hallik**

One of my earliest memories is of sitting cross-legged on the floor, the massive *Whole Earth Catalogue* splayed across my lap. I was five years old and lived in the tiny college town of Grinnell, Iowa.

Images of DIY geodesic domes sat next to seed kits, discussions on permaculture, and nascent technologies. I immersed myself in it with endless curiosity. While the images that then seemed indelible have faded, the ethos behind them remains deeply instilled in me: community, possibility, vision, and the need for novel multidisciplinary solutions to serve a common purpose.

This formative influence was one of the inspirations for the company I founded roughly thirty years later and now lead as CEO, Another Tomorrow. It is a company built on a vision to reinvent fashion as a system and bring it back within our planetary boundaries through innovation, a rigorous commitment to sustainability, collaboration, and creative business models that treat clothing as an asset. However, what happened in the middle was just as important.

'ChemLawn,' water on fire, and metal detectors

From Grinnell, where my father was a professor and my mother an artist (who also happened to do a stint at Exxon), in 1987 we moved to the (larger) college town of Meadville, Pennsylvania, in the northwest corner of Pennsylvania. Meadville is home to Allegheny College, where my father had accepted a job, and to a once-thriving industrial landscape – part of America's 'Rust Belt' – that was experiencing the bottom falling out.

The college was a fascinating place. I first lost myself in the natural environment of the campus, playing in the brooks and trees, and later in the hotbed of ideas and access to culture from visiting scholars and art-

* CEO, Another Tomorrow

ists. I took classes there while still in high school and immersed myself in whatever I could get my hands on. My mother ran the local arts council, a multidisciplinary cultural center incorporating a gallery, theater, and dance studio housed in the space above the town's central marketplace. I took classes there throughout my childhood, and my mother put me to work assisting her with administrative tasks while she wrote the grants that funded the council's work. This is also where I had my first contact with Eastern philosophies through a local Tai Chi master, who opened my mind to new ways of understanding our place in the world.

The town was also emblematic of the ravages of unchecked capitalism. Chemicals were everywhere. While my mother held firm against it, nearly every other lawn in our neighborhood was sprayed routinely with toxic chemicals to kill off weeds, accompanied by little flag warnings to keep children and pets away for days. Lake Erie, a short drive away and one of the Great Lakes (collectively responsible for 20% of the world's freshwater supply), was routinely closed to the public, still suffering from algal blooms and toxic waste. We were not far from the Cuyahoga River, which famously had caught fire two decades earlier, in 1969, one of the watershed moments that galvanized public support for the creation of the Environmental Protection Agency and Clean Water Act.

While a multifaceted environmental crisis was in full swing and nascent stages of serious policy interventions were taking hold, the bottom was also falling out of the economy around the college. Once home to the largest zipper manufacturer in the world and a halo of tool-and-die factories, well-paying industrial jobs disappeared year after year as factories continued to move overseas. There were no evident programs for retraining. No major new employers emerged in their wake. The social fabric, held together by dignified work and reliable, solid pay, began to tear. In the three years in the mid-1990s between when I started middle school and my younger sister did, a metal detector was installed at the school's entrance, with backpacks banned in favor of clear plastic bags that were easier to search. An epidemic of drug abuse has taken hold that has led deaths by overdose to more than quadruple by the end of the 1990s.

My experience in Meadville was replete with confronting evidence that the system of unchecked capitalism was not working – not for the environment, not for ecosystems, and not for people.

Early access to tools

While the environment and social fabric were evolving (or devolving) around me, I was immersing myself in early access to one of the tools that would come to shape humanity and profoundly impact the world economy in the decades to come – the internet. My father had become involved with NeXT computer, the company founded by Steve Jobs between his stints at Apple. NeXT was aimed at the higher education market and ended up being used at CERN to develop the world's first instances of a web server and browser. It was thrilling to have access in our basement to the very first instances of the web. I saw the immense power of technology as a tool for communication and the transformation of a wide swath of disciplines as this was taking place right before my eyes in its use at the college. My father instilled in me that this was just the beginning of a transformative era and encouraged me to enroll in computer science in high school, where I learned to code.

Building off that mind-opening influence of the Whole Earth Catalogue, these years began to impart in me a sense that the overall economic system had to evolve if people and the planet were to flourish and that technology, policy, and culture all have a critical part to play. The seeds were sown for my conviction that we can reimagine and create a different collective future if we focus on collaboratively solving system problems at the intersection of disciplines.

Life intervenes

My final years of high school and my college years, between 1997 and 2003, were wrought with pain and significant pivots. My parents divorced, a decision my sister and I would have welcomed years earlier, except that it ended up splitting us up; I moved to Columbus, Ohio, with my dad to finish high school. My sister and mother moved to Pittsburgh, Pennsylvania. The fabric of our family started to tear, and I buried myself in my studies, among other less wholesome teenage activities, as an escape. I headed west to Berkeley, California, inspired by its cultural leadership. I was pulled between interests in architecture, which I saw as uniquely situated at the intersection of disciplines with a profound tangible influence on the environment and people's lives, and economics, a field I fell in love with my last year of high school as a way of understanding the powerful global dynamics that shape our lives.

At the end of my first semester in college, while literally walking out the door of my father's house to begin the drive home to my mom's, the phone rang, and we received the news that my mother had taken her own life, the culmination of years of mental illness at a time when treatment was poor and discussion taboo. The ground felt like quicksand, and everything shifted. I switched schools, transferring to Cornell University, and gave up on architecture in favor of economics, which I thought was better suited to supporting myself financially as it became evident that this would be critical. I became highly pragmatic, and without even noticing I buried much of the creative influence my mother had imparted to me alongside the pain of her memory. While retaining my interests in the environment and policy, my focus became squarely on getting a good, stable job.

When the policy fellowships I applied for my junior summer were roundly met with rejection, I decided to join the herd at the career center and apply for the finance jobs so many of my classmates were pursuing. Given my curiosity to explore the world and my strength in economics, I could see how I might fit into a role in foreign exchange or emerging markets. The banks saw this as well, as they took interest in my work co-authoring a paper on electricity pricing in the Environmental Economics department at Cornell. A fifteen-year career in finance began that summer on the trading floor of Morgan Stanley in the foreign exchange business.

Fifteen years in finance

After a summer spent in research, I wanted to get in on the action and had the perfect opportunity when one of the senior leaders concluded that I would make an excellent options trader. I agreed with the trading part as it came naturally to me; however, I found options trading to be a narrow field, and over the years I continuously searched for opportunities to build things. I quit three times (the second time to pursue a degree in Energy and Environmental Policy) and cut my teeth as an intrapreneur building and leading various businesses in emerging markets. I also steeped myself in the organization to maximize every opportunity to make an impact, joining the board of the Morgan Stanley Foundation as a trustee, representing the company at the Council on Foreign Relations, building public school mentorship programs within the division, and leading the Philanthropy Committee.

On the surface I was thriving: I became a Managing Director in 2016, the uppermost rank in title at the firm – an achievement of importance to me in proving myself as a woman, and a woman in trading, where gender disparities are particularly stark. Deep within, however, I was not at peace with myself and felt increasingly disconnected from the core of my upbringing despite the immense respect and appreciation I had for the institution where I was working. I had a front row seat to capital being allocated in massive amounts across the financial services industry, including to companies with high levels of negative externalities – from coal mines to palm oil plantations to the meat packing industry – as well as to governments with poor environmental and human rights records. It was, and largely still is, how the system and its incentives worked. I felt deeply that there was a more humane and future-relevant way to allocate capital.

Finally, in 2017, I summoned the courage to make a move from emerging markets to ESG. My first stop was internal, as the company had stood by me and given me immense opportunities for personal and professional growth. When there wasn't an immediate full-time role in which to develop my vision, I took a sabbatical.

Down the rabbit hole

When I embarked on my sabbatical, I told myself I would use the time to explore opportunities and educate myself with open-minded curiosity and avoid making any immediate decisions on new roles. This did not happen. Within six weeks two things occurred: I was met with an opportunity to help build out an ESG business in emerging markets with another firm, and I had begun my descent down the rabbit hole of exploring the massive negative externalities of the fashion industry. The former was exactly what I thought I wanted, but the latter had my attention.

Most of what I had unearthed in my research into other industries was familiar to me: fossil fuels, energy-intensive automotive and aviation industries, waste, water, and chemicals issues in the food industry. However, what I found in fashion floored me. The massive impact at the level of emissions and waste (over half of clothing ends up in landfill within twelve months) was just the beginning. I began to see a broken economic model of "take, make, waste" requiring massive margins to offset the immense inherent risk and a drive to lowest-cost production that took a huge toll on environmental, human, and animal welfare in many of the same ways as food and petrochemicals, fashion being either an agricultural or petrochemical product, or often, both.

I could not unknow what I learned and turned toward the opportunity to become a part of the solution. I wanted to bring a fresh vision for how the fashion industry could begin to transform itself and operate within our planetary boundaries and with respect for the vast value chains on which it depends.

At the same time, I began personally investing in early-stage companies in climate tech, materials science, and sustainable consumer goods that I believed had promise to transform the categories and cultures in which they operated. This gave me an even stronger conviction of the power of capital to transform and provided me with a lens into the world of entrepreneurship that I was about to enter.

Another tomorrow

When I began my research into how I could make an impact in the immense landscape of fashion, I put my former finance hat on – focusing on scale and technology. What I quickly realized was that new tools needed takers and that there was very little appetite for systemic change. This was in 2018, when ESG was still considered a "nice to have" and the senior leadership of the biggest brands were turning a blind eye to new business models such as resale, hoping they would go away.

I saw that the industry needed a new vision for how brands could operate, one that was commercially scalable and more economically resilient, as a case study for ambitious and holistic change. Then I set out to build just that.

Another Tomorrow exists to model a new future for fashion as both an end-to-end sustainable luxury brand and a re-commerce platform. Fundamental to the company is the idea that clothing must once again be treated as an asset – made to last and with infrastructure to support a life cycle across multiple potential owners. Starting out, I knew literally one person in the industry, but with the support of a few early, generous connectors I quickly navigated to industry insiders unsettled by the footprint of their work. They joined forces to help me learn and assemble a remarkable team, and we set out together to take "farm to table" to "farm to closet" with traceable, sustainable supply chains. We leveraged technology to create digital twins for our products, set a new standard for supply chain transparency and authentication for re-commerce, and built a best-in-class in-house resale program. We have since further innovated in our supply chains by developing "just-in-time" manufacturing capabilities to create resilient, demand-responsive production.

At the time of writing, in 2023, we are three and a half years old, the first Certified B-Corp in our field with customers in over forty countries. We have also looked beyond the impact of our company, focusing on pre-competitive collaboration on policy and innovation that will help lift the industry, and creating a case study for the future of fashion.

My experience in building Another Tomorrow has reinforced my faith in problem-solving at the intersection of disciplines, in systems thinking, and in collaboration. I have taken inspiration from solutions from other industries such as automotive (just-in-time manufacturing and resale) and food (farm-traceable, regenerative supply chains), and at every turn I have met people hungry for the opportunity to contribute to transforming this industry. This has been true from sheep farms in Tasmania to organic cotton fields in New Mexico, from textile mills in Italy to partners in materials science using algae and bio-waste in labs, to our technology collaborators with whom we are pioneering new circular business models. In all cases, people (and their companies) are most able to contribute creatively and take care of our societies and planet when they and their families are safe and financially secure, further reinforcing the inherent co-dependencies between people and planet.

Every day it is a privilege to do this work. It is often challenging, always rewarding, and full of evidence that impact happens everywhere, most often in roles where the word 'sustainability' features nowhere in the job description. It has also brought me home to my full self, reigniting connection with the creative world of my mother, unleashing healing, and tapping into a much broader and deeper well of vision – a process that has brought me a deep sense of peace after many years of blocking out this part of me.

I encourage anyone interested in leading the world into a more compassionate, resilient, and sustainable place to just start from wherever you are, to bring your full self to your work, and to operate with curiosity, collaboration, and the vulnerability to share your vision. We all need you.

44 Five waves

*Victoria Hurth**

I suspect that no one starts life with a burning desire to commit themselves to a purpose, to make a meaningful contribution to the greater good. But I *do* believe that this desire is waiting to be nurtured inside all of us. And while my generation (Gen X) was born at a time both horrifying and wondrous, we can choose to find our purpose. We can choose to make a stand.

Throughout my career, my purpose has been to bring organizations into alignment with the idea of long-term wellbeing for all (what, in other words, we would call *sustainability*). And I have pursued this purpose across a wide array of pathways and projects: working in London inside some of the biggest companies in the world; being director of a social enterprise pub; heading up environmental expeditions in Ghana; being Associate Professor of Marketing and Sustainable Business; a board director; helping run a food-waste charity; supporting the United Nations in developing Sustainable Development Goal business target 12.6.1; facilitating consensus-building between seventy-seven countries and twenty-five international liaisons to create the world's first international standard in governance of organizations (ISO37000); leading the world's first National Standard in Purpose-Driven Organisations (PAS808); and – becoming an impact advisor for Una Terra VC and SACE in 2023.

In these many and varied positions, I've honed my specialisms – governance, marketing, leadership, and culture – describing myself as an independent 'pracademic' (a practical academic).

For many years I've been guided by a desire to act, asking myself: What is the most impactful thing that needs doing, and that I can uniquely help with? This approach has made my life one of full and forward momentum. When choices were tough, I asked myself how I'd look back on this moment in years to come.

---

* Independent Pracademic

This helped me to face the facts, to plot a course – even if it meant living out of a backpack, moving away from what I felt was wrong until I found what was right.

I think of my journey as being formed of waves of insight. These waves represent breakthroughs – of new ways of thinking and acting. Each breakthrough helped to sharpen and refine my purpose, setting out new approaches – and systems – to get to where I most wanted to be.

What follows, then, are the five 'waves' that have shaped my journey and helped to define my purpose.

The first wave: Adults are strange

My first wave started with all the thoughts and feelings I had when I was very young. I grew up aware of how happy I was and how amazing my parents and brothers were. My life was overflowing with joy, even if we had few material 'things.' This meant I *knew* that wellbeing was not about consumption or fancy schools. This was an important first step in my journey.

From a young age, I was told – and believed – that I could achieve anything. I was allowed to question everything. Where my mother belonged to the political left, my granddad – who lived with us – belonged to the political right. My mum was full of academic wisdom, and my dad of practical insight. We debated. A *lot*. I tried to become a vegetarian at the age of four, and after my parents found rotten meat hidden in cupboards, they gave in. I was brought up as a Catholic, which for me meant a keen sense of being a global citizen with no more right to life than anyone else. It gave me a sense of deep empathy for those I had never met.

In the mid-1980s, when I was thirteen, I felt my first conscious wave of insight. Tuning into the conversations of adults beyond my family, listening to their hopes, dreams, and advice, I was shocked to find that these reflections almost always revolved around buying things and doing things, such as going to university or getting a job, to buy yet *more* things. Deconstructing advertisements from a young age – guided by my mother – taught me that the adult world holds some very strange assumptions, and that the economy – and marketing – play a powerful role in shaping how these adults see and experience the world. More importantly still, I knew that it didn't have to be this way. Naive and cocky, I saw that the world could change, that it needed my help. I still do.

The second wave: Humility

My journey took me to university, buoyed by a desire to understand and fix the world. I studied business, spending a year in industry as a marketing coordinator for a 3M advertising adhesive. Frustrated, bored, and lacking agency, my next strategy was to get to the heart of business decision-making.

Accenture was my route, and at the age of twenty-one, I was taking part in head office conversations in a range of large global corporations. How I managed to stay for three years I still don't know, but it was the perfect place to achieve my *second* insight: the humility of realizing that no matter how strong my purpose, I am only human. The 'system' would change me before I had a chance of changing the world itself. I committed then never to get out of bed knowing my energy would make the world a worse place, helping those with lots of money to make more of it at the expense of those that didn't. I had to get out, and quickly. I grasped an alternative path – in international development, volunteering in a small township charity in South Africa.

The third wave: The veil of ignorance drops

I faced my next turning point in 2002. The World Summit on Sustainable Development, held in Johannesburg, was in full swing, with business leaders from around the world gathered to address our unsustainable economy. I remember Busisiwe Mkhwebane distributing booklets and me picking up one by the Henrich Böll Foundation called *Fairness in a Fragile World*. Every page was a revelation.

I realize now that my life, as for many, had been hidden behind a thin veil, keeping me apart from the urgent challenges the world was then facing: biodiversity loss, soil erosion, climate change, inequality, a lack of social cohesion, and water scarcity. When the veil dropped, the world began to make more sense. I was now on a deliberate journey to connect my amateur observations to the real world, out there.

The fourth wave: Learning my way to solutions

This period was disorientating. The more I unlearned and learned, the further I moved from the 'normal' world around me. I didn't know what to do with this insight, but I steered close to my course – continuing to learn, to engage. I knew I would find the answer.

This 'course' took me from a master's degree in Environment and Development at the University of Kwa-Zulu Natal to a PhD at the University of Exeter in Sustainable Consumption. I opened every disciplinary and practice 'box' I came across – psychology, sociology, anthropology, economics, marketing, education, engineering, art, biology – trying to connect the dots and to make sense of them, and resisting all pressure to specialize to advance my career.

It was then that I realized two vital things: that the world needs 'boundary spanners' who see very broadly and can move between 'worlds,' and that it needs independent actors who act for the collective good.

This gave me the breadth and depth of understanding I lean on today, but this wave wasn't complete until I had absorbed what this all meant for me as a *human*. I recognized the unjust, mindless obliteration that our planet is facing, of all the intensely beautiful places, people, and species that are at risk. I wept a lot and faced the worst. I carry this with me as a source of strength. I know I have nothing to lose and that I can always, always, work to make things better.

The fifth wave: Arriving at insights I can lead for

I didn't intend to go into full-time academia. This period supercharged my knowledge about the worldviews that underpin our 'business-as-usual' economy. Going back to the early macro-level work of Daly, Meadows, and Brundtland, it became clear that while it is easy to complicate sustainability, much of what is wrong and where we are trying to head is quite simple.

The goal of the market economy is purpose-driven: the allocation of resources to optimize overall wellbeing. More than that, this goal is the same as the definition of sustainability, especially if we reword Brundtland's perspective on the meta-purpose of humanity: wellbeing (not just any old thing) for all (not just a few) and for the long term (not just for now) – long-term wellbeing for all.

The problem we face relates to the way in which we have organized the market economy to achieve *this* goal, conflating wellbeing with financial income (GDP, profit, and wages) and making business a myopic bit-part focused primarily on profit maximization. In all of this, society's best interests, and the social and environmental systems that underpin it, remain out of sight and off the balance sheet. It remains ungoverned.

If you exponentially grow such a system, it will inevitably result in existential threats to our collective long-term wellbeing. In trying to achieve 'sustainability,' we have focused on isolated elements of the strategy ('the three pillars'), but not on the goal of long-term wellbeing for all the people that these pillars support.

This is why we need to think transformationally, leveraging a way of thinking that has been bubbling away, globally, for years. We need to lean into a coherent and shared agenda. When I look around me today, I see people using different languages to ask for and bring about the same thing.

- Macro: a wellbeing economy (not GDP).
- Meso: operationalized by purpose-driven organizations (not profit maximization).
- Micro: powered by humans doing meaningful work (not the highest-paying roles).

This may feel radical, but as the unsustainability crisis closes in, the alternative is losing the democratizing and innovation benefits of a market economy and moving instead to command and control.

And this is not a theoretical argument. When we stop to notice the things around us, we can see that the transition is already underway. Changing the status quo – of laws, norms, and 'language' – is a collective endeavor. It will take *all* of us to effect change. This is what underpins my leadership as an independent clarifier and amplifier for the world.

And once this new way of thinking becomes our reality, I will happily celebrate my redundancy.

45   Lessons from a career supporting social entrepreneurs: Five levers of change

Yasmina Zaidman*

The first time I visited Kibera, an informal settlement in Nairobi, Kenya, I had a hard time wrapping my head around the many challenges faced by the people living in the community, including poor housing construction, open sewers, crime, and low rates of formal employment. I arrived with the goal of inspecting toilet projects that had been set up to address the complex sewage challenge that the community was facing. But these projects were dependent on outside donors, who were few and far between. A few years later, I visited Mukuru, another informal settlement near Nairobi, to meet with the Sanergy Collaborative, a rapidly expanding company that was providing high-quality sanitation to local communities.

The non-profit impact investment organization that I work for, Acumen, had invested in the Sanergy Collaborative precisely because of its circular economy solution, an innovative methodology for creating value from waste. While visiting the settlement, I saw the *opposite* of dependency, with local teams solving problems and doing it at scale. Acumen supported this project based on our understanding that for-profit businesses can play a role in solving some of the greatest challenges associated with poverty. The Sanergy Collaborative is doing exactly that: creating value, creating access, creating dignity.

What drives actual revenue for the company – which has kept access to sanitation as affordable as possible – is the conversion of waste into organic fertilizer that supplies 8000 farmers. In the process, they've created nearly a thousand jobs.

In its work, the Sanergy Collaborative has set out to tackle the complexities of poverty relief using the tools of business. But it is much more than a sanitation and fertilizer business. They listen to their customers and value their employees, particularly those who are most often overlooked. What's

* Chief Development and Partnerships Officer, Acumen

more, the leadership team is gender-diverse and is composed primarily of Kenyans, while the workforce itself is drawn from underemployed youth in the communities they serve. Sanergy works with a wide cross-section of funders and investors, recognizing that the problems they are solving live at the intersection of market opportunities and public goods. Throughout their business model, they engage the local government as an ally to ensure there is widespread access to sanitation. I believe that Sanergy's approach offers a blueprint for what it will take to address the social and environmental challenges we are facing as a planet.

My experience working across non-profit, for-profit, and hybrid models for social and environmental justice has shown me that there is no one way to change the world. I've learned that arguing about the *right* way will ensure that our circumstances worsen rather than improve. Instead, I believe that we need to work with multiple levers for change, which must be deployed in combination to accelerate progress toward a just, sustainable, and resilient world. These are the five levers that have guided my work in social impact so far.

Democratize leadership

In the 2010s, Majala Mlagui was leading a social enterprise that linked artisanal miners in Kenya to their markets. They achieved this by improving their mining practices and working to make the industry more ethical and transparent. Through this work she learned about the kinds of policies that could either help or hurt the livelihoods of vulnerable mining communities and was invited to help shape these policies based on her knowledge of the issues on the ground. After joining the Acumen community as a fellow in 2013, she found a group of peers grounded in an ethos of moral leadership. They gave her the confidence, a few years later, to run for office as Deputy Governor of one of Kenya's forty-seven regional governments. Later, she told me that having a cohort of leaders who believed in her was what she needed to pursue her candidacy and become Kenya's youngest-ever elected Deputy Governor. Her story shows what is possible when proximate leaders work together to change the conversation.

It is time to shift the conversation, to move away from the idea of *what* leaders should do to consider *who* should be leading. Real change requires new voices, new perspectives, and new kinds of skills and experiences. And I don't mean this in a tokenistic way, where a few representative local leaders are brought into leadership forums to create the appearance of diversity and inclusion. Instead, we need actual shifts in the people who set the agenda and make decisions. Wherever possible, I try to elevate voices that are often overlooked or ignored, lifting perspectives that offer a different view. I create teams, events, and strategies that value inclusion, driven by the belief that this is what will lead to the best outcomes, and humbled by the fact that I am able to lead in the first place.

Understand (and sometimes question) markets

When I first joined Acumen in 2003, I was tasked with finding companies that deliver safe drinking water and sanitation to low-income communities. I had heard statistics about the high toll of waterborne diseases, and the enormous time and physical burden of transporting water that women bore. What I didn't understand was the deep failures of both governments and markets when it came to providing something as basic as water and a toilet.

This realization struck me when I visited a community in India that had recently gained access to safe water through a company that I had invested in as head of Acumen's Water & Sanitation Portfolio. The company appeared to have everything figured out; people wanted access to clean, healthy water, and they wanted it to be conveniently packaged in water cans that could be delivered to their homes. But there was a catch. Prior to this company's arrival, water was 'free.' For many in the community, low-quality, inconvenient, but free water was better than paying a fee, especially among the poorest.

For the company to succeed and reach the desired level of consumption within the community, making their company viable, they had to invest significant time – more than a year – working closely with the community to demonstrate the benefits of treated water. Even then, they found that their water treatment systems needed to be subsidized to be accessible to *everyone* in the community.

For us to create social impact at scale, it's critical that we understand how markets work. But markets are made up of people, and market failures are often a sign of a much deeper problem. A well-functioning market requires access to information, and a degree of trust. If consumers have been previously disappointed by a new product or service that would supposedly benefit them, introducing another new product with claims about those benefits is extremely difficult. Ultimately, market-based solutions are only part of the answer. On issues like access to basic goods and services such as water, sanitation, healthcare, education, and electricity, I have witnessed the most successful market interventions take root where local and national governments are playing their part as well – providing access to information, subsidies where needed, and an enabling environment for entrepreneurs to operate.

Unlock capital

I joined Acumen because it refused to accept the notion of choosing between impact and profitability. Acumen was determined to find a path that would achieve both while always being honest about the trade-offs that can result from putting people and the planet first. Impact investing has been gaining momentum in recent years as investors consider social and environmental factors alongside financial returns. According to the Global Impact Investing Network (GIIN), the estimated size of the global impact investing market reached $ 715 billion in assets under management in 2020. Other estimates of how much is invested for impact vary widely, from the International Finance Corporation's estimate of $2 trillion to even higher numbers cited by private research firms.

The bottom line is, there's a lot of money out there looking for impact, but definitions of impact vary widely. As Kusisami Horberger explains in his book *Scaling Impact: Finance and Investment for a Better World*, diverse, local, and early-stage enterprises still struggle to get their first investment, and many social enterprises encounter repeated rejection. Meanwhile, the impact investing sector is expanding at an estimated 9.5% per year according to an Allied Market Research 2023 figure. To meet the scale of impact required, the question isn't only how much capital is needed, but also *where* it is going.

Unlocking capital for enterprises that offer breakthrough solutions to global problems will require new tools for investing. But they'll also require a willingness to question assumptions about the right rate of return for investments that are solving social problems. I've seen great things happen when investors come together in blended finance vehicles, when governments work together with investors to support enterprises during their early start-up years (de-risking them for later-stage investors), and when grants and donations are used to catalyze entrepreneurial ecosystems and support social enterprises seeking to scale through investment.

The key to unlocking capital is unlocking human creativity, using capital for much more than just creating *more* capital. There's never been a better time to question and disrupt the uses of capital in the name of building a more just and sustainable economy.

Partner like the world depends on it (because it does)

The notion of radical collaboration is closely tied to the creative uses of capital. There's not a single entrepreneur, government, investor, or donor that can single-handedly solve the complex challenges we face today. When we work together, in coordinated ways, it becomes possible to achieve things that were previously considered out of reach.

When I first observed the growing momentum around the off-grid energy sector, back in 2015, it occurred to me that we could do something much bigger than simply finance companies as they came through our pipeline. As far back as 2005, we had begun to build an ecosystem of companies involved in delivering energy access to low-income customers across India and East Africa, bringing lighting and small-scale electric grids to people who had little to no energy access.

But it was a conversation with Liz McKeon, Director of Programme, Planet & Head of Portfolio, Climate Action at the IKEA Foundation, that changed everything. She asked: "What could we do together that would be truly catalytic?" This conversation launched an unprecedented partnership that would expand our energy work. It enabled us to learn from our investments about what it would take to solve the problem of energy poverty once and for all. Eventually, it would extend beyond Acumen and the IKEA Foundation to include corporate allies such as Autodesk and Signify, government partners such as the United Kingdom's FCDO (Foreign, Commonwealth & Development Office) and the Netherlands' FMO (Entrepreneurial Investment Bank), global networks such as GOGLA (Global Off-Grid Lighting Association), and even individuals and family foundations – all united under a shared goal of bringing energy access to those living off the grid. Our partners pushed us to take bigger risks, to share hard truths, and to deepen our impact wherever possible.

This taught me a crucial lesson: that *who* you partner with is as important as what you aim to achieve together. Helping Acumen build the muscles for partnership has been my focus ever since, and I encourage others to ask themselves: How can I be a better partner, and whom could I partner with that shares my goals?

Lead with love

I have had the benefit of being mentored and inspired by Acumen's founder and CEO, Jacqueline Novogratz, as well as our President and COO, Carlyle Singer, who joined Acumen in 2013. These two extraordinary leaders have helped Acumen fulfill its potential as a global organization with strong core values and proximate leadership operating across the world. Having strong female mentors and role models has made all the difference in my life, and when I realized roughly ten years ago that I was able to pay it forward, I set myself a new challenge – to empower others to express their creativity and passion for change.

Leadership is often defined based on power and wealth. But the people who've inspired me have chosen other metrics of success. Specifically, they have chosen to listen, to empower others, to act with compassion, and to create positive social change – especially for those who have been marginalized or exploited.

Pursuing this model of leadership requires a set of behaviors that are difficult to define, so I will share a story instead. Theresa Njoroge was falsely imprisoned in Kenya because she refused to pay a bribe. She spent two years in jail with her young daughter. While there, she could have simmered in resentment at the injustice she had experienced, but she chose instead to listen to the other women that were there alongside her. She listened to their stories and the circumstances that had brought them to prison. She decided that when she left prison, she would work to help women who had been imprisoned – for the crime of being poor – to rehabilitate their lives, allowing them, once again, to contribute to their families and communities. This led to the creation of Clean Start, an organization that has served thousands of women in Kenya.

Inspired by women such as Jacqueline, Carlyle, and Theresa – who choose to lead with humility, compassion, and love – I have chosen to lead by investing in others. Whether it's the extraordinary entrepreneurs and local leaders that I have had the privilege of supporting or the amazing women that I mentor, their leadership gives me the greatest hope that we can build a world that works for everyone.

By focusing on these levers for change – inclusive leadership, market understanding, creative capital, bold partnerships, and leading with love – I meet each day with the confidence that real change is possible. Together.

Conclusions

Luca Zerbini[*]

A new type of capitalism

My generation (Gen X) was brought up worshipping libertarian capitalism, particularly as it meant opposing the utopia of autocratic communism. The exhilarating postwar European reconstruction and booming economy that our parents experienced in the 1950s and 1960s were soon tempered by the Cold War between the United States and the Soviet Union in the 1970s and 1980s, which meant fighting for freedom and democracy against dictatorship and oppression.

We were in love with the United States, with the American dream and the opportunity to have it all and have it now. The industrial might and automation of the West made almost any product innovation immediately affordable to the middle class, and consumerism fed its economic engine, giving the opportunity of prosperity to millions of people in the Western world. There was a lot to like about those years in Europe, when entire nations that had been fighting two global wars and devastated an entire continent were brought out of poverty by the Marshall Plan, finding renewed economic success and building a peaceful collaboration that would federate them around the ideal of a European Union, finally set off in the 1990s.

We were cheering for value creation and freedom, a double motivating message to fall in love with.

Milton Friedman, with *Capitalism and Freedom* (1962), became the spiritual leader of free markets in the 1960s, supporting the policies of US President Ronald Reagan and UK Prime Minister Margaret Thatcher, and focused the purpose of corporations on "shareholders above all," making financial return the only metric to evaluate the success of a company, while GDP became the only parameter to measure the achievements of a country, and cash was the only way to evaluate individual accomplishments. Wall

[*] Co-Founder & CEO, Una Terra Venture Studio

Street became the modern equivalent of the Agora of ancient Athens – but now all the debates could be won simply by throwing more money on the table, rather than with eloquence, logic, or dialectic.

From leveraged buyouts, epitomized by Henry Kravis and George Roberts in the famous business book *Barbarians at the Gate*, fueled by the rising junk bonds of Michael Milken, as depicted in *The Predators' Ball*; from commodity funds betting they could corner entire markets, such as LTM Capital in *When Genius Failed*, or trade their way to billions of dollars, like the hedge funds of Steven Cohen in *Black Hedge* or Nassim Nicholas Taleb in *Black Swan*; from the mortgage-backed financing breaking risk management rules in *The Big Short*, to quantitative traders like Jim Simons, the "Man who solved the Market", generating money based on purely mathematical algorithms, independent of the real underlying economy … Every 'financial innovation' considered 'making money' as the destination rather than the fuel required to get there (i.e., the outcome rather than the by-product of a well-run business). All of this happened under the watch and with the full support of the powerful monetary policies of central banks, wishing to fuel larger financial bubbles in order to oversee a longer period of expansion instead of dealing with politically hard-to-manage moderation or self-discipline, pushing the envelope until another financial crisis or depression would eventually hit.

Hollywood reinforced the message and made it a global mantra: "Greed is good" was the scream of Gordon Gekko to Telda Paper shareholders in the 1980s movie *Wall Street*, and plenty of others echoed his message by showing as ideal the life of *Dallas* or the equivalent version for the younger generation, *Beverly Hills 90210*. And, of course, the *Mad Men* of marketing and advertising were singing to the same tune, using the infinite power of the press, TV, and later social media to replace the world war restraints of our grandmothers in the name of convenience and consumption. They replaced the door-to-door milkman with his refillable glass bottles with the convenience of lighter, single-use plastic bottles containing any combination of water, sugar, and chemical flavors, easier to carry and throw away after a picnic. They convinced us that we should eat meat every day as 'fast food,' even if it required industrial cattle farming at scale, bad land use, and significant health risks for animals and humans; or that we should change outfits at ever faster rates with 'fast fashion,' to the point that a new shirt produced in Asia and delivered to our door was less expensive than washing the old one and could come in any color combination to follow the latest fashion trends. The common denominator is that if you are rich, you should show it with your car, your plane, your house, your clothes, and your luxury items, and everyone will admire you for your success and will be attracted to you – regardless of the consequences for the environment or society. Silicon Valley helped accelerate the rate of technological innovation, making it easier to leave behind the last electronic gadget or iPhone version for the newer one, and creating even more waste in the process. They sold us the idea that tech could solve any issue and make us more productive at no cost. And they made us addicted to social media, software, and artificial intelligence, losing touch with our local reality in search of the virtual perfection of impossible friends and perfectly crafted unreal stories.

We were leveraging more to buy a house or lease the car we could not afford *at a family level*, or to show financial results we could not achieve organically *at a company level*, and to keep people happy despite reasons to believe there was a need to tighten our belts and spend less *at a country level*. Central banks pumped billions into our economies to extend our 'positive momentum' and we started at all levels to borrow from the next generations to keep our hunger satisfied: financially, with ballooning deficits and national debts; and environmentally, with 'Overshoot Day' moving from December to June and for some countries consuming the equivalent of two or three planets a year.

Sustainability and impact investing

Yet, over time, something started to feel wrong. We started hearing that even people who had become millionaires or even billionaires were still not happy or did not feel successful. Our infinite growth agenda started clashing with the abundant but limited resources of our planet, and the obsessive pursuit of money was conflicting with mental and physical health. The top diseases in the Western world became obesity and mental illness. Scientists started warning us about upcoming climate disasters; we watched *An Inconvenient Truth* with Al Gore, democratizing global warming for the first time, and *The Blue Planet* with David Attenborough, depicting the microplastics disaster resulting from uncontrolled and uncontrollable waste. Documentaries such as *Food, Inc.* and *Seaspiracy* talked about how we were killing animals by the millions, destroying forests to raise crops to feed them, and using way too much of our water in the process, not to mention using chemicals to fertilize them, polluting entire food chains and eventually ourselves.

If the failure of communism can be dated to the fall of the Berlin Wall in 1989 and the subsequent disintegration of the Soviet Union and many socialist countries in the 1990s, capitalism continued undisturbed, absorbing all resources and time to produce always more and more, exerting its influence well into the 2010s and 2020s.

But just to be clear, this is not an anti-business book, or even an anti-capitalist book. This is instead a book showing there is another way – a way that everybody is looking for, and one that will positively impact all of us, all our companies, and the planet on which we live.

Think about the energy transition to *renewable energy*, which would allow continued growth but using "infinite and free" resources such as the light of the sun, the force of the wind, the water of our rivers and oceans, and the power of the energy inside the earth. It would also limit conflicts between countries that own fossil fuels and those who use them, as energy would not depend on such fuels and would be more widely distributed and available to all. Or think about the *circular economy*: the very essence of our initial focus at UnaTerra is to turn unsustainable solutions into sustainable ones, reusing multiple times the same materials without undermining the sources of ingredients or supplies that we have been using (and stressing) for decades. Or think about *healthier food alternatives* that do not consider animals just as nourishment for humans but leverage lab growth or precision fermentation as more sustainable processes; or *regenerative farming*, which eliminates chemicals and combines old practices (e.g., crop rotation between nitrogen-fixing crops such as soybeans and nitrogen-hungry ones such as corn) with more recent ones (such as cover cropping, that is, planting living roots after a cash crop is harvested to avoid erosion, increase water retention, and improve soil health).

There is a way to pursue long-term wellbeing for people and the planet at the same time, and this is the economic system and impact investing approach more and more people find sensible and want to be part of. We call it 'regenerative economy,' and it is superior to other prevalent systems as it takes into consideration the needs of investors, but also those of employees, customers, suppliers, and notably the environment. It considers not only financial or manufactured capital, but also social, human, and environmental capital, and all of them can be quantified and become part of the profit and loss and of the balance sheet of a corporation.

The previous system may still sound more appealing to some people in the short term (or maybe they just follow the incentives they have been given without wondering if they are sensible not only for themselves but also for the rest of the world), but it cannot be sustained in the long term, and it would not allow humans, animals, and plants to coexist for many generations to come.

Regenerative economy and impact investing instead promise to balance all needs, to allow continued growth, but a balanced growth that can be sensible and exciting for everybody, at global, country, group, and individual level.

Purpose and meaning for the next generations

Ever since I was a boy, I have loved nature. I recall asking my dad to get me a membership to the World Wildlife Fund and to National Geographic, which I proudly displayed in my room. My brother and I were lucky to have parents who loved traveling and spending time with us, so we had the opportunity to visit many countries around the world with them. Seeing the national parks in the United States or going on safari in Kenya, visiting the Amazon forest in Brazil or diving in the Galapagos in Ecuador, swimming in the Maldives or exploring the Philippines in Southeast Asia, just amplified my love for nature and the amazing planet we live on.

So, after my formative business years, which were fully focused on growing businesses to make more money than my competitors, I moved back to Europe from the United States midway through my career. I knew that beyond my passion for growth and innovation, I had to find a purpose and a calling to a higher mission, and 'naturally' I went back to *my love for the environment and the world around us*. I first worked on emissions reductions for cars, where I learned how technology and regulations could drive immediate change and value. *There was no trade-off between financial results and sustainability*, if we could leverage innovation to replace 'dirty' solutions with 'cleaner' ones, and as long as someone cared (or was required to care by legislation). Being successful on the market would then mean also being impactful environmentally, and the two could go hand in hand.

After my wife and I had our first son, I decided to tackle another challenging space – packaging – where I learned how collaboration across the value chain was key. I was with the Ellen MacArthur Foundation right from the start of the New Plastics Economy program and we were able to federate all value chain actors, align them to a common Global Commitment, and work in a noncompetitive environment to share solutions to fugitive plastic waste. Even if the issues are still far from resolved, the combination of research, regulation, innovation, and collaboration across industrial players and infrastructure, as well as consumer awareness, accelerated the progress and allowed for the generation of significant value on the market.

I then started to take up board positions to have further impact in other relevant areas, such as lighting efficiency and smart buildings, as well as sustainable food and personal care. Across all these industries, Europe was leading the charge on the environmental and social side, with most other regions replicating its model and solutions with some adaptations and a few years of delay. With the passage of US President Joe Biden's Inflation Reduction Act in 2022, together with the scientific might of its research hubs and the smart capital of Silicon Valley, the United States has started to pick up the pace, even if it is still focused mostly on the energy transition for climate change mitigation, rather than embracing the full spectrum of investment opportunities to reduce carbon footprint and biodiversity loss, as well as addressing head-on the increasing divide and inequality that are fostering continued social issues, ignoring and neglecting diversity, equity, and inclusion.

After the birth of our second son, I was frustrated as I felt my (lack of) time was limiting my impact. I realized that only by leveraging dedicated capital and experienced people could I exercise a wider influence. And I continued to think, could I look my sons in the eye and serve as an example in twenty years, when they ask me: "What did you do to stop all of this?"

Hence, with the support of my family and the guidance of my coach, I was able to take the decision to leave my corporate life after more than twenty-five years of work and start my first true entrepreneurial endeavor, creating a 'portfolio life' that could maximize my impact across multiple areas.

We made many mistakes, but we also spent a lot of time learning and putting together the best possible people – in our team, in our board, in our impact committee, and as our partners. It was an incredible period of learning, of taking calculated risks, of working incredibly hard, of testing our limits, and of drinking from the infamous 'fire hose' while trying to keep calm externally.

The incredible women in this book have helped me significantly along the way, and they have helped Una Terra VC Fund (of course, together with many men too). But it felt right to thank women first, as they are fighting an uphill battle in our society, and they still find the time and commitment to do what is right, to try to save our planet, our environment, and ultimately ourselves from climate change and biodiversity loss, and in doing so, they are the true leaders of this age.

I believe the stories and women of this book will show us the way, which eventually will lead the world out of this environmental crisis. While men such as Jeff Bezos, Elon Musk, and Richard Branson still spend billions looking at infeasible solutions to relocate on a different planet, these incredible women continue to show us that the solution is here, in the most beautiful home we could have ever hoped for, if only we can protect it and nurture it like they do every day, rather than treating it as an infinite resource to take advantage of and to abuse at will.

Their inner fire and motivation will never be extinguished, and they will eventually replace the real fire and risks of climate change and biodiversity loss and bring back nature and our planet, our 'Una Terra,' to its original beauty and magnificence.

So, thank you for joining us with this reading: We look forward to having you on this journey as well!

Closing

Katie Alcock[*]

One way to open your eyes is to ask yourself, "What if I had never seen this before? What if I knew I would never see it again?" - Rachel Carson, *The Sense of Wonder*, 2011.

The stories in this book chart the often-unconventional routes of forty-five women into the world of sustainability. For some, their stories are tied to their childhood experiences in nature; growing up in the pastoral idyll of the Italian countryside or making a solemn promise to 'save the dolphins'. For others their story begins later, in a search for meaning and greater purpose. A pseudo-spiritual 'eco-awakening' or an 'aha' moment helps to tell a good story, but the move towards sustainable thinking is often incremental and then unshakable. The more we see of the world, whether through balance sheets and audits, research reports or by crossing continents, the easier it is to refuse to be complicit in its destruction. This is happening on the streets, as people around the world protest the multinationals and governments that prioritize profit over people and planet. And in Europe, radical concepts like degrowth are starting to creep in from the political fringes. We know that the old system is broken, and we need to rebuild it.

To create a socially and environmentally just world it is critical that women have a seat at the table. Although the impacts of the climate crisis are felt more acutely by women than men, they are poorly represented in international climate change discussions and decision-making roles. We were all reminded of this when the photo of the almost all male cohort of world leaders at COP27 made the rounds after the conference. The women in this book have all dedicated themselves to making the future possible, so let's amplify their voices and make space for the next generation of climate leaders.

[*] SB+CO